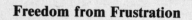

Freedom from Frustration

FREEDOM FROM FRUSTRATION

HARDY R. DENHAM, JR.

BROADMAN PRESS
Nashville, Tennessee

Dedicated to My Children:

Mary Denham Walker and Gary
Ruth Denham Barger and Dean
and
Stanley Ross Denham

my

"Gifts from the Lord"

4252-96
ISBN: 0-8054-5296-6

Dewey Decimal Classification: 152.4
Subject heading: EMOTIONS

Library of Congress Catalog Card Number: 81-65827
Printed in the United States of America

Contents

1

Mercy, Am I Frustrated!

Frustration!

It's found everywhere!

Time and time again people say, "Mercy, am I frustrated!"

A housewife had a nervous breakdown during a Sunday-morning service in her church. She had gone to church overwhelmed with frustration and tension from a week of housework, shopping trips, managing a budget, tending to children, plus the bombardment of countless television and radio commercials. Sitting in church with her nerves all shot, she heard the choir sing, "Awake, my soul, stretch every nerve." That did it—that was too much!

Can anything be done about frustration? Is there an answer for this dark cloud which frequently hovers over our lives?

The self-help section in bookstores offers many titles on a variety of subjects and contains books dealing with many themes related to frustration. Yet, I've never found a definitive book on frustration. The fact is, I'd never even thought of trying to write a book on the subject of frustration until it was suggested to me. But why not a book on this subject? Every human being is frustrated at times—and some all the time!

The word *frustration* comes from the Latin, *frustra,* and it means "in vain." The dictionary furnishes us a definition of frustration: "a sense of insecurity or dissatisfaction arising from unresolved problems or unfulfilled needs." That definition covers a wide territory in only a few words. There are all kinds of problems in life. Some of these problems defy solution. We feel frustrated when we face a problem but can find no solution for it. Furthermore, all of us have needs—all kinds of needs. We feel frustrated when we have the experience of our needs being unfulfilled.

Dr. Maxwell Maltz wrote: "We feel frustrated when we fail to achieve important goals or to satisfy basic desires."[1] This statement adds still another dimension to the fact of frustration. We experience it when we fall short of any projected goal or purpose in life.

Harold Walker defined frustration as: "The experience of blundering into dead-end streets and blind alleys and getting nowhere for all our trying."[2] He added, "You and I may as well face the blunt fact of frustration as one of life's inevitables. There is no escape from it, and sooner or later we are caught in its grip."[3]

Psychologists classify frustration in three main categories. These are environmental, personal, and conflict.[4] Our environment is filled with factors which thwart us in a variety of ways. The weather interferes with some planned activity or a vital machine fails to operate properly. The result is that we become frustrated. Personal frustration relates to our individual goals and relationships. This area of frustration is the most painful of all, and it is usually the type of frustration we have the most trouble resolving. Conflict frustration involves the activity of choosing.

Daily we face choices and must make decisions. This fact of life can produce its own breed of frustration.

The Scope of Frustration

The first fact which can be established about the scope of frustration is that all of us experience it. Dr. Maltz writes, "Everyone feels frustrated now and then because of our imperfect natures and the complex nature of the world."[5] So, all of us, regardless of our station or rank in life, live from time to time in the twilight zone of frustration.

Even the Lord Jesus Christ experienced frustration. Jesus was frustrated in service and with his disciples. His hometown of Nazareth wouldn't accept him (Mark 6:1-6), and his disciples were slow to understand the true nature of his kingdom (10:33-36). There can be no doubt that the Lord showed frustration over Peter with these words, "Get thee behind me, Satan: thou art an offence unto me: for thou savourest not the things that be of God, but those that be of men" (Matt. 16:23).

Some of these frustrations we experience can affect our ego. The frustration arising from failure, or the experience of coming out second best in sports, scholastic, or business competition can produce feelings of insecurity, lack of self-esteem or worth, and the loss of social approval. This type of frustration is extremely painful.

The second fact which can be established about the scope of frustration is that it can be experienced in virtually every area of our lives. This is true because in all these areas we have needs, face the potential of problems, and desire to reach some goals. There is:

The frustration of failing;
the frustration of having too much to do
    in the time available;
the frustration of having to do what we
    don't want to do;
the frustration of losing out in a highly
    competitive society;
the frustration experienced in marriage
    and family living;
the frustration of poor health or a lin-
    gering illness;
the frustration experienced in daily work;
the frustration of having to choose;
the frustration of constant change and
    changing adjustments;
the frustration created by a gadget- and
    machine-dominated life;
and the frustration of trying, and trying,
    and trying again when everything
    seems to be so hopeless.

The list could continue ad nauseum.

Not only is frustration experienced in virtually every area of life, it is also expressed in a variety of ways. The emotion of anger, the feeling of regret, and the spirit of despair can all be expressions of frustration.

The Seriousness of Frustration

Since frustration is a fact of our corporate and individual lives, we need to learn about its nature. Is frustration a normal part of the wear and tear of daily life which we must learn to accept and live with? Or is frustration a fact of life which is both unavoidable and yet correctable? I believe it is the latter. No one of us can avoid feeling frustrated because we deal with unsolved problems, experience unfulfilled needs, and have unreached goals. But we can do something about frustration, which is what this book is all about.

Not only can we do something about frustration—we must do something. Frustration is related to stress, and stress can be a serious matter. In fact, frustration and stress are inseparable. Even though stress includes more than frustration, frustration is a form of stress.

The proof of this is found in a bit of self-examination. How did you feel the last time you were frustrated? The frustrated person is not calm, composed, relaxed, and at ease. Even though one may appear outwardly undisturbed, inwardly there is something ranging from a simmering unrest to a raging tempest. The point is: the frustrated person is experiencing stress to some degree. Psychologist Floyd L. Ruch wrote: "When any goal-directed activity is blocked, the normal individual experiences a psychological and physiological reaction which continues as long as the need remains unsatisfied."[6]

The stress of frustration, or frustration-stress, can be dangerous to your health. To be sure, some stress is essential for living. A person needs a certain amount of stress to keep going. This is even true of frustration-stress. The feeling of frustration has a certain amount of survival value, for it can motivate a person to overcome the obstacles he encounters. Instead of resigning and giving up when frustrated, some of us try just that much harder. Yet, a prolonged state of frustration-stress can be dangerous.

Medical doctors have identified various results of stress. Dr. Mario Pineda says, "The pituitary gland signals the adrenals to increase production of adrenaline. The blood pressure goes up, the pulse rate increases, the respiration rate is increased, the tone of the muscles increases and peripheral circulation decreases causing a cooling of the extremities." Dr. Pineda adds that "any organism that maintains a sustained level of stress response wears down faster. They become easier targets of difficult medical problems that are directly related to excessive and continuous levels of stress."[7] Some physicians state that between 50 and 80 percent of all diseases are stress related. Dr. S. I. McMillen listed fifty-one diseases under ten different categories which are caused or aggravated by emotional stress.[8]

The physical results of prolonged stress, including frustration-stress, are serious in themselves. Added to this is the damage that may be done to relationships which are involved in our frustration, plus some very undesirable emotional spin-offs from frustration.

Unresolved frustration can lead to anxiety. Anxiety is defined as more than simple worry. It is a general feeling of apprehension. "The characteristic behavior patterns of an anxious person are those of unhappiness, restlessness, unaccountable moodiness, mood swings, irritability, and dissatisfaction with self and others."[9]

Frustration can also lead to hostility and aggression. Psychologists call this the "frustration-aggression hypothesis." Paul H. Landis wrote, "Block a person's activities or wishes, and his natural reaction is to fight, to attack the sources of frustration."[10] Gary R. Collins expressed it like this: "Whenever people get frustrated they have a tendency to respond with aggression. This aggression can be of two types. Sometimes we react *overtly,* lashing out with our tongues or maybe with our fists. This is like blowing our horn at the train. Such behavior isn't usually acceptable in polite society, so it is more common for us to react *passively.* Here we may smile and be charming on the outside while we seethe with anger inside and look for more subtle ways to express ourselves."[11] This feeling of hostility, and the aggression it can produce, often leads to serious consequences in the area of interpersonal relationships.

So, the seriousness of frustration can be seen in the fact that it is a form of stress. Some stress, including frustration-stress, has a detrimental effect upon the body. When it is unresolved, frustration can lead to life-paralyzing anxiety and relationship-damaging hostility and aggression.

The Solution of Frustration

Certainly the recognition of what frustration is, and what it can do to us and those with whom we are involved in life, should motivate us to do something about it. But what? The person who says, "Mercy, am I frustrated!" often asks, "But what can I do about it?"

Many people do the wrong things in an attempt to resolve their feelings of frustration. One of the most common errors in dealing with frustration is to hide it with drugs. In the early 1950s, the psychotropic drugs were introduced, and our society was changed overnight. These drugs have the effect of calming people down without dulling the brain or hindering their ability to engage in daily activities. These drugs have the ability to reduce anxiety, combat depression, relieve or prevent fatigue, create a sense of self-confidence, take away tension, eliminate insomnia, and reduce the level of hostility or agitation one feels.

A few years ago I went to a physician with symptoms which were like an ulcer, but gratefully it wasn't. Responding to my symptoms, the doctor began treating me as if I had a duodenal ulcer. A small, white pill was prescribed to be taken four times daily. "What's this for?" I asked. The doctor answered, "It'll take the edge off what's bothering you." I later checked a pharmaceutical journal and learned that the pill is a tranquilizer—a drug designed to relieve my tension and stress. I might add that I've since quit taking it.

However beneficial these stress-relieving drugs may be, they never solve anything. I'm not indicating that such drugs aren't helpful and even needed in cases where people are extremely distraught. They can help a person get through a crisis, but as Gary Collins aptly writes, "If they prevent us from facing our stresses and simply obscure our problems, then drugs are being misused."[12]

Drugs don't change our environment. The disturbing stimuli are still there. We may be able to recognize them intellectually, but we don't respond to them emotionally. Added to this is the fact that these drugs can become habit-forming. Even though a drug may not be powerful enough to cause physical addiction, people can and do develop a *psychological* addiction.

The most dangerous drug of all is alcohol. Millions of people seek to resolve the frustrations of life by drinking. Many persons observe the daily cocktail hour to unwind from the stress and tensions of the day. One beer commercial seen frequently on the television announces that when you have finished with a hard day's work, it's time to go to your favorite bar and have a beer. Drinking alcohol may give a sense of relaxation and well-being in which the frustrations and anxieties of the day are forgotten, but the situations producing these are still there. Furthermore, this form of escape from frustration can ensnare, as the rising degree of alcoholism in America tragically proves. Roger Crook wrote:

> The person who uses alcohol to escape from a way of life which he finds painful is taking a medicine that may destroy him. . . . The person who drinks to escape a difficult situation, whether he drinks moderately or to excess, does not by that action remove his difficulty. Although he may find some temporary relief, he does not solve his problems. If his problems are at home, he complicates them rather than helping. If they are at work, they are there when he returns no matter how much he drinks. If the problems are within himself, his drinking does not resolve them or make him any more satisfied with himself. However much a person may need to relax, he will find a permanent solution only by confronting his problems head-on.[13]

Besides the use of drugs (alcohol is also a drug), people seek to resolve frustration in other ways.

Among these are hypnosis and the relatively new Transcendental Meditation (TM) movement. Both of these create a state of relaxation and thus effectively alleviate many of the stress symptoms of our fast-paced society. The problem with these, and other such techniques, is that they are attempts to escape or temporarily evade the realities causing frustration-stress, and that isn't the answer. How, then, can we properly deal with frustration?

I believe that frustration must be faced head-on. Escape techniques don't solve the situation—they just prolong it. However, I don't believe there are any pat answers or simplistic solutions for frustration. It seems to be a characteristic of our times to develop capsule philosophies which are easily prescribed as simple solutions to all our problems. But frustration is far too complex for such a simplistic approach.

Since frustration is related to so many different areas and factors of daily living—environment, personal, and conflict—the discussion of solutions must be reserved in some degree for an examination of some of those particular areas and types of frustration. I shall attempt to do this in other chapters as we look at the feeling of hopelessness, the facts of failure and regret, the reality of anger, the frustration of constantly choosing, the stress we experience in home relationships, as well as others. Each different area of frustration will dictate in some degree its own solution.

Let's understand that, even though frustration is unavoidable and experienced in all areas of daily living, it is correctable. We can do something about it, and in doing so we will become more of the persons the Lord God wants us to be.

Conclusion

So many times we all say, "Mercy, am I frustrated!" All of us experience this, and we experience it in virtually every area of life. In fact, I've discovered that writing about frustration, and attempting to offer some help to those who are troubled by it, has caused me to experience frustration! I say with you, "Mercy, am I frustrated!"

Notes

1. Maxwell Maltz, *Creative Living for Today* (New York: Pocket Books, Gulf & Western Corporation, 1967), p. 83.

2. Harold Blake Walker, *Power to Manage Yourself* (New York: Harper & Brothers, 1953), p. 64.

3. Ibid., p. 65.

4. Floyd L. Ruch, *Psychology and Life,* Sixth Ed. (Chicago: Scott, Foresman & Company, 1963), p. 201.

5. Maltz, *Creative Living for Today,* p. 83.

6. Ruch, *Psychology and Life,* p. 202.

7. Mario Pineda, "Stress: A Little Dab Will Do You" (*The Clarion Ledger-Jackson Daily News,* April 20, 1980, Section E, p. 1).

8. S. I. McMillen, *None Of These Diseases* (New York: Pillar Books, 1975), pp. 61-62.

9. Elizabeth B. Hurlock, *Adolescent Development,* Fourth Ed. (New York: McGraw-Hill Book Company, 1973), p. 52.

10. Paul H. Landis, *Your Marriage and Family Living* (St. Louis: Webster Division, McGraw-Hill Book Company, 1969), p. 35.

11. Gary R. Collins, *You Can Profit from Stress* (Santa Anna, CA: Vision House Publishing Company, 1977), p. 39.

12. Ibid., p. 186.

13. Roger H. Crook, *How to Be Nervous and Enjoy It* (Nashville: Broadman Press, 1975), p. 115.

2

When Life Seems Hopeless

There is an Oriental fable which tells of a man being pursued by wild animals. In his flight from the animals, the man stumbled and fell over the edge of a deep pit. He reached out, grabbed hold of a root protruding from the side of the pit, and held on for dear life. The snarling animals waited at the top of the pit.

The man looked down and discovered to his dismay that the bottom of the pit was filled with venomous vipers. Hanging between the animals above and the snakes below, the man became aware of a gnawing sound. He discovered that a gopher was chewing away at the root onto which he was holding. Talk about a hopeless situation!

The threshold of my office door is crossed with disturbing regularity by people who are frustrated with life. These people wear the various faces of frustration. The causes of the frustration they experience are almost as diverse as the people, but the sense of hoplessness they exhibit and express is basically the same.

Some of the reasons for the frustration experienced by people will be dealt with in subsequent chapters of this book. The focus of this chapter isn't on the problems or situations of life which can produce frustration, but on the outlook on life the frustrated person often has. In the state of frustration the person can come to look on life as hopeless. Even though the condition of being frustrated may have been prompted by only one or more happenings or situations, the end result can be that the waves of the emotion roll outward to wash on all the shores of one's existence. In such a state a person can come to feel that life itself is hopeless.

The novel, *The Broken Year* by Richard Brickner, is about a young man confined to a wheelchair for the rest of his life as a result of an accident. The young man asks his attendant, "Do you think I have a future?" The attendant answers, "As a pole-vaulter, no; as a man, yes."

The daily wear and tear of life with its routine monotony can cause a person to feel hopeless. The dreaded diagnosis that an illness is terminal, or the loss of a loved one, can cast the shadow of hopelessness over life. Problems for which there seem to be no solutions, the pressure of business, and a world situation with its constant tensions can leave a person feeling hopeless. When several of these factors converge on a life, that sense of hopelessness can be overwhelming.

The people who cross my office threshold wearing the many faces of frustration ask, "What can I do when life seems so hopeless?" This chapter is an attempt to answer that question. I recommend that we refuse to be negative, review the situation, and resolve to do something.

Refuse to Be Negative

It's so easy for us to become negative in our thinking. This is especially true when life is clouded with frustration and hopelessness. A person can become negative about himself, seeing himself as a failure, incompetent, or just a plain nobody. Leslie Weatherhead told of finding a boy wandering alone amid the ruins after a German bombing raid of London. Weatherhead asked the boy where his family was. The boy replied that they were all dead. Weatherhead asked, "Who do you belong to?" The boy responded, "I'm nobody's nobody." Some frustrated people feel that way.

A person can be negative about the situation which produced his frustration. Frustrated by the demands of his job, a person can call it a rat race that leads nowhere. Frustrated in marriage, a person can become so negative in thinking that he looks for the quickest exit.

Furthermore, a person can become negative about God. Job in the Old Testament wasn't the first man, or the last, who felt that God was against him. Job lamented,

> "If my troubles and griefs were weighed on scales,
>   they would weigh more than the sands of the sea,
>   so my wild words should not surprise you.
> Almighty God has shot me with arrows,
>   and their poison spreads through my body.
> God has lined up his terrors against me" (Job 6:1-4, TEV).

Many people have reacted to the crises of life by crying out, "God, what did I ever do to you to make you treat me this way?"

Because frustration so easily produces negative thoughts, the first step in combating the feeling of hopelessness is to assume a positive posture. To be sure, this is not easily done. This is especially true when the sky seems awfully dark. Added to that is our natural inclination to look on the dark side and expect the worst to happen.

A boy came home from school and told his father, "Dad, I think I failed my arithmetic test today." The father, desiring to teach the boy to be a positive thinker, said, "Son, think positively." The boy responded, "All right, Dad, I'm positive I failed my arithmetic test."

We can be positive about life and its experiences for there is something good in the worst of situations. Robert H. Schuller wrote about a woman who came to talk to him about divorcing her husband. He asked her if the man beat her, refused to work, was a drunkard, homosexual, narcotics addict, or unfaithful. To each question the woman answered no. The pastor then advised, "Well then, be careful before you divorce him. I know a hundred lonely women who will run after him as soon as you let him go."[1] That woman was not as bad off as she thought.

Being positive when we are frustrated is essential, for only then can we begin to turn the tide of our emotions. Attitudes are more important than facts. Karen Horncy made the following distinction between a psychotic and a neurotic: "A psychotic is a person sho says, 'Two plus two is five'; that is, they are completely out of touch with reality. A neurotic, however, is a person who says: 'Two plus two is four, but I do not like it.' There is something about the way life is put together that does not suit them."[2]

The English author E. M. Tomlinson wrote, "The world is what we think it is. If we can change our thoughts, we can change our world." We are controlled by so many factors in this world. But the one thing over which we exercise complete control is our thoughts. When we feel pushed into a corner by life, we can give in to negative thoughts, or we can exercise thought control and be positive.

Review the Situation

Most situations in life are not as hopeless as they sometimes seem. A motorist crossing a bridge saw a man climbing over the railing, obviously about to take his life. The motorist stopped his car and got out shouting, "Wait! Don't jump!" The motorist raced over to the man at the rail and said, "Life can't be that bad. Let's talk about it." So the two men spent the next few minutes talking and then both jumped into the river!

Humorous as the story may be, the fact remains that life situations are not as hopeless as we sometimes think. Overreacting to a tense and frustrating situation is a common tendency many of us have. We blow things out of proportion. That a situation isn't as catastrophic as we think is a fact we can see if we'll take time to honestly review the situation.

A business had fallen into a serious slump. Sales were off. The president of the company secured the services of a business consultant to study, evaluate, and recommend what could be done to correct the situation. After his study, the consultant asked that all the company sales personnel be called to the home office for a meeting. The consultant showed the sales personnel a big sheet of paper which had a black dot right in the center. He then asked them what they saw. The people began to answer, "There's a spot on the paper." "There's a black mark on the sheet." "There's a dark mark in the center." The consultant turned to the president of the company and said, "Sir, that's what's wrong with your company. All your people saw was the dot in the center of the page. None saw all the clean, white space around the dot." There are things in life which are not to our liking, but look at all the good that is there.

To analyze all aspects of the situation which led to your feeling of hopelessness, you must be careful to do two things. First, be sure you recognize the real cause of your frustration. People tend to vent their frustration and hostility on people and things who aren't to blame. Psychologists call this displaced aggression and scapegoating. "Often an individual directs his hostile feelings toward some object or person other than the one actually causing his frustration. . . . The clerk who snaps at his wife and children because he failed to get a raise is using his family as a scapegoat."[3] Even little children do this—they slam doors when they're mad at their mothers.

Furthermore, look at the source of your frustration in relationship to the whole of life. Life can be described as a house with many rooms. Merely because something isn't right in one room of the house of life doesn't mean everything is also wrong in the other rooms. By taking into consideration other areas of life and their importance and blessings, one can realize that the cause of frustration may not be all that major. "Most of us, however, allow ourselves to be thrown 'off course' by very minor or even imaginary threats, which we insist upon interpreting as life-or-death or do-or-die situations."[4] We release a dollar's worth of adrenaline over a dime's worth of aggravation.

This review of the situation can lead to the discovery of possible solutions. Some poet wrote:

> For every evil under the sun
> There is a remedy, or there is none;
> If there be one, seek 'till you find it;
> If there is none, never mind it.
> (Author Unknown)

Two words of advice are pertinent in discovering workable solutions for the feeling of hopelessness. First, *elim-*

inate those solutions which will sow the seed for even greater frustration later on. The medicine can be worse than the sickness.

The "Amos and Andy" series was one of my favorites. One of the characters was known as the Kingfish, and he was always bothering Andy. One day Andy said, "I've put dynamite under my vest. The next time the Kingfish slaps me he's gonna get his hand blowed off."

Some of our solutions create even greater problems for us. For example, one recent study of divorced people reveals that they are even more unhappy than they were while married.

Second, *in discovering a solution for frustration, depend on God for help.* The Lord is the Creator and giver of life. Since frustration and the sense of hopelessness it can breed is a life problem, God can help. "There are little storms raging inside all of us, ministers and counsellors and psychologists included, that threaten to sweep us away if we don't call in the Master of wind and wave."[5] The wise man of old recommended, "Trust in the Lord with all thine heart; and lean not unto thine own understanding. In all thy ways acknowledge him, and he shall direct thy paths" (Prov. 3:5-6).

Resolve to Do Something

The final remedy for the feeling of hopelessness is up to the person. The ancient city of Ziklag was given to David by Achish, king of Gath. During the absence of David and his men, the city was invaded and destroyed by the Amalekites. The people were taken captive. Frustrated by their own losses, David's men spoke of stoning him. The Bible says, "David was greatly distressed . . . but David encouraged himself in the Lord his God" (1 Sam. 30:6). It is obvious that David had divine assistance in dealing with the frustration of defeat, but he also did his part. David refused to surrender to despair.

Everyone faces some situation in life which causes frustration. The problem for many is that they lack the resolve to do anything about the frustration-causing situations. They complain about their frustration, but do nothing to resolve it. An old proverb advises, "It is better to light a candle than to curse the darkness."

There is an unusual young man who is a patient at the Methodist Rehabilitation Center in Jackson, Mississippi. His neck was broken playing high-school football. He is completely paralyzed as a result of that injury. However, this young man gets around in an electric wheelchair which is guided by lung power. It's called the Sip and Puff. By blowing or sucking through tubes he is able to steer the chair. His social worker says he has a better attitude than any patient in the center.

This young man resolved to do something about a situation which produced more than mild distress. He could have resigned himself to spending the rest of his days in bed. Instead, he determined to do what he could, and in doing so has become an inspiration and example to others.

The remedy for the frustration may mean acceptance of the situation. If we can't alter the difficulty, we can alter ourselves to meet it. As the above-quoted poem states, for some problems there may be no remedy other than simply changing your attitude and accepting the situation. A plaque on my office wall contains Reinhold Niebuhr's "Serenity Prayer":

> God, grant me the serenity to accept
>   things I cannot change,
> Courage to change things I can change,
> And wisdom to know the difference.

There are situations which are beyond our power to change. Wholesome living then dictates acceptance, rather than continued resistance. Floyd L. Ruch wrote: "An attempt to overcome a frustrating obstacle may be impractical. The best course of action then may be to leave the frustrating circumstances and find a situation where satisfactory adjustment *is* possible. The frustration of giving up a goal is often less than that of repeated failure."[6]

A World War II veteran was seen hobbling toward a religious shrine in the French Pyrenees Mountains. The veteran had lost a leg in the war and was going to the shrine to pray. A skeptic standing nearby saw the man and said, "What's he going to do? Ask God to give him his leg back?" The veteran overheard the man and answered, "No, I'm going to ask God to give me the strength to live without my leg."

There are times when the only solution is acceptance. When a person accepts a frustration-producing situation, rather than resisting it, he then puts himself in a frame of mind to discover how the bad situation can be used for good.

A young bride from the East Coast followed her husband to an army camp located on the edge of the desert in California. The only housing available was a rundown shack near an Indian village. The heat was unbearable in the daytime—115 in the shade! A hot wind blew all the time, and dust covered everything. The young wife's days were long and boring, and her only neighbors were Indians, none of whom spoke English.

When the husband was sent off for two weeks of maneuvers, the bride became so despondent she wrote her mother that she was coming home. She couldn't take it anymore. The mother's response was a quotation from Fredrick Langbridge:

> Two men look out through the same bars:
> One sees the mud, and one the stars.[7]

The wife decided to accept the situation and look for the stars. First, she made friends with the Indians. Then she began to study the desert and discovered it to be beautiful. She learned about its past and plants. She became such an expert on that area that she later wrote a book about it.

What had changed? Not the Indians. Not the desert. She had. By accepting the situation which had caused frustration, she transformed her circumstances.

Conclusion

The Boston Marathon is run in April each year. The course is 26 miles, 285 yards long. About 2,000 people sign up each year to run in the endurance race. Not all of these finish the race. What defeats most of those who drop out is a hill about six miles from the finish line. It's called "Heartbreak Hill." That's where most quit, gasping, "It's hopeless."

Life has its Heartbreak Hills. They are situations which produce such frustration that some people give up, moaning, "Life is hopeless." This isn't true even though situations do prompt feelings of frustration.

It is my conviction that there is hope when frustration makes us feel hopeless. There is, if we will refuse to be negative, review the situation, and resolve to do something.

Notes

1. Robert H. Schuller, *Move Ahead with Possibility Thinking* (Garden City, NJ: Doubleday & Co., Inc., 1967), p. 71.

2. John R. Claypool, *Growing Up and Going On* (Printed sermon, Northminster Baptist Church, Jackson, MS, October 5, 1980).

3. Floyd L. Ruch, *Psychology and Life,* p. 207.

4. Maxwell Maltz, *Psycho-Cybernetics* (New York: Pocket Books, 1974), p. 221.

5. John D. Jess, *Coping with Anxiety* (Grand Rapids: Baker House, 1973), p. 28.

6. Ruch, *Psychology and Life,* p. 203.

7. Frederick Langbridge, *A Cluster of Quiet Thoughts* (Published by the Religious Tract Society).

3

If at First You Fail . . .

His business suit was stylish and impeccable. From the top of his modestly groomed head to the toes of his polished shoes, he was the picture of Mr. Successful American. I couldn't help but think, *certainly he has no problems*. Why had he sought counsel? It was a while before he finally got over his discomfort at being in a pastor's office and stated the reason he had come. Hesitantly he said it, "Pastor, I feel like a failure."

It took a little prodding to open the gate. When it did this man, a picture of vibrant success, let flow a tide of frustration born of failure. He was at mid-career. The visions of success he had possessed at the beginning of his climb to the top had vanished. He knew he would never reach his goal of becoming the senior executive in his firm. His life at home was characterized by tension and stress. He and his wife lived in different worlds with few common interests, and his children had adopted life-styles which he abhorred.

He expressed his feeling by concluding, "All these years, all this work, and for what? Only to fail!"

That man is a composite of many people I've encountered in my work as a people helper. Most of these were not lazy people who tended to think that the world owed them something. Instead, they were busy people—people who had dreams, ambitions, and hopes and were not afraid to work long and hard to make these come true. But all of them experienced failure in some area, endeavor, or relationship of life.

Failure is one of life's universals. It is an experience all persons have in common. Occasionally I hear and read the words of those who have a "pop theology." They claim, among other ideas, that man was created to succeed. The first man was also created perfect, but he ruined that in the Garden of Eden. It is impossible for any one of us in our imperfect condition to live a life which will be completely free of mistakes and failures.

There are institutions in society whose existence is predicated on human failure. Hospitals minister to people experiencing health failures. Prisons are for those who have failed in relation to the law. Insurance companies help people who have property failure. Divorce courts are for couples who have failed in marriage. The welfare system helps people who have experienced an economic failure.

Even the most successful and famous men in the world have experienced failure. In one sense, every great accomplishment and significant achievement has been won at the price of failure. The success ultimately experienced was not instantaneous, but the end result of repeated attempts, many of which ended in failure.

Thomas Alva Edison was probably the greatest inventor of all time. He well knew the meaning of failure. One of his teachers called him "addled," and his headmaster said Thomas "would never make a success of anything." His inventive successes were the results of countless experiments and attempts which ended in failure. Albert Einstein was a poor student in high school and failed the entrance exam at Zurich's Polytechnic Academy the first time he took it. Winston Churchill twice failed the entrance exam for Sandhurst.

These were men who made tremendous contributions to mankind, but who also experienced the agony of failure. Richard Dugan remarked, "I have a suspicion that those who have never felt like a failure have also never tried anything."

Failure is one of the many causes of frustration. To be sure, all of our failures do not necessarily produce frustration. Each day we fail in little ways that hardly give us a moment of emotional pain and are quickly forgotten. However, failure frustrations, or the frustrations born of failure, can be some of our greatest and most dangerous frustrations. Is there freedom from this? Or is one doomed to spend the rest of one's days in the agony of defeat under the cloud of frustration? If at first you fail, what then?

Trying to discover help in dealing with failure frustration, I have found three exercises which are of value.

Be Positive in Attitude

The most important factor in a time of failure is how you feel about it. What determines whether failure becomes final defeat or is just a stepping-stone to ultimate success is the attitude you have about it.

Consider two contrasting examples of attitudes in failure at the 1976 Olympic Games in Montreal. When their yacht came in fourteenth in a field of sixteen, two young British sailors set fire to the boat, left it burning, and waded ashore. They didn't win the race, or even come close to it. What was worse, though, was the fact that they failed in losing because of their attitude in defeat. On the other hand, Olneus Charles of Haiti didn't win the 10,000-meter race. He didn't even come close to winning. He was lapped nine times in the race and finished five minutes behind everyone else. But Charles didn't stop running—he didn't quit. Even though he failed to win the race, he had an attitude that made him a winner in his failure.

Failure can plunge a person into deep despair. The greater the degree of failure, the greater the failure frustration, and the greater the possibility of despair.

What do people do when they have that failure feeling or experience failure? Some feel sorry for themselves and begin to lash out at anyone and everyone. Then some try self-justification, seeking to absolve themselves of any and all blame for the failure. Others search for a scapegoat. They transfer the blame for their failure to someone else. Finally, there are those who just give up and quit. All of these are negative responses to failure, and none of these helps remedy the failures experienced.

The only way to deal with failure in a remedial fashion is to have the right attitude in failure. The second and third steps suggested in this chapter for dealing with failure frustration are predicated on the mental exercise involved in this first step. It is necessary to be positive in attitude. This means that you refuse to accept your failure as final. No failure is ever final unless and until it is accepted as that.

Be Perceptive in Understanding

When a person experiences failure and the frustration it breeds, he needs to take time to analyze it carefully. There are several things a person needs to understand about his failure if he is to change it into success.

First, *understand that there is a difference between failing in some activity and being a failure.* To fail doesn't mean you are a failure. What you are as a person is always more than what is involved in one activity or endeavor. Maxwell Maltz wrote, "You may make a mistake, but this does not mean that you *are* the mistake."[1]

One of the most important things about you is your self-image or how you see yourself. If you see yourself as a failure, you will fall into the pattern of acting in a manner commensurate with that self-image.

So, the first thing you must understand in dealing with failure and its frustration is: to fail in some performance doesn't mean you are a failure as a person.

Second, *determine if the failure feeling is really justified.* Many times we have that failure feeling when, in truth, we haven't failed. I have a friend who feels she has failed to make a good grade on every test taken in college. When the grades are posted, my friend is usually in the "A" category. Thus what was *felt* to be failure is not that at all.

Often we allow other people to project their standards of success and opinions of failure on us. Sometimes our failure feeling is the result of peer pronouncements about our ineptitude or lack of achievement.

One of the cardinal commandments in America today is "Thou shalt not fail!" In the minds of many it really doesn't matter what you must do to succeed, but just don't fail! Having written this new commandment, some people then set up standards of success by which we are judged to be successful or unsuccessful. But, are they right, especially when other people disagree with them?

I went through a difficult time professionally a few years ago. Our church was in a building campaign and matters weren't going well at all. Naturally the spirit of the church was affected. There were those who placed a lion's share of the blame at my door. After conferences and meetings with these, I went home with a sense of personal failure. Just as I was ready to accept the blame and agree with their assessment, some member of the church would call, write, or come to say, "Pastor, you're doing a great job and we appreciate you." Understandably my emotions were like the pendulum of a clock, swinging one way and then another. I recovered my equilibrium in that time of gravitating from the failure feeling to the success syndrome by taking a long, hard look at the standard by which I was being condemned and commended.

My experience is an example of the fact that we can feel like failures and be judged so by others when, in truth, we aren't, at least not as much as we or others may think. When you feel you have failed, stop and see if you really have. Your feelings, though real, may not be justified.

Third, *recognize that you may have asked to fail.* That sounds a bit ridiculous, but it's a fact of life. Some of us actually set out to fail. One way we do this is by attempting something we aren't qualified or equipped to do. Just because we may think we can do something is no sign that we have the abilities the task demands.

A young man enrolled in a theological seminary. He testified that one day he looked up and saw two large letters etched in the clouds—the letters "PC." He accepted this as a sign from God that he was to "Preach Christ." After taking the I.Q. and aptitude tests, the seminary dean explained, "Son, I am inclined to think that the letters in the sky really meant 'Plow corn.' "

Each one of us has limitations. Because of these we cannot do some things that might interest us, neither can we do the best in everything we do. A person who attempts a task that is beyond the scope of his ability is asking for failure. The failure that results is the outcome of an attempt that shouldn't have been made in the first place. We must accept ourselves and comprehend both our limitations and our capacities. If we keep our limitations in mind, we can spare ourselves many failures by not attempting deeds outside the range of our abilities.

Added to this is the fact that at times we have also asked for failure by expecting it. A friend remarked that our expectations tend to become our experiences. If you attempt something you are capable of doing, but with a sense of inadequacy and the opinion that you will probably fail, the chances are . . . you will.

One major key to success in any endeavor is to view yourself as successful. The mental image has a profound effect upon the exercise. Maxwell Maltz has pointed out that our attitude at the beginning of an endeavor has a bearing on the outcome of it.[2] George Weinberg wrote, "If you believe that you have any ability at all, and if you let that belief move you to try to achieve something, your confidence will grow, and because confidence itself is an asset, your chances of achievement will increase."[3]

Fourth, *accept the blame for your failures.* Often this is the hardest thing of all for us to do. I pointed out earlier that two common negative responses to failure are the attempt at self-justification and scapegoating. Since the Garden of Eden, man's response to failure has been to excuse himself and attempt to "pass the buck" to another. All of us have experienced the tendency to do this, and at times the tendency is carried out. The truth is that we won't begin to travel the road to recovery from failure until we are ready to honestly say, "I failed and I accept the responsibility for it."

A couple had experienced twenty-five years of matrimonial misery. Their life together was an experience of nearly constant tension which made the achievement of intimacy virtually impossible. She was resentful of the time he gave to his business and felt that his only interest in her concerned her body and not her soul. He was resentful of the fact that she steadfastly refused to be the lover and ego-builder he needed.

Thus, year after year their marital experience was more *martial* than anything else. It was only when the husband realized that he had put his business before his family, and then changed his priorities, and his wife accepted the blame for her failure to understand his needs and minister to them, that the two began their recovery from matrimonial failure.

Fifth, *learn the lessons that failures can teach*. One of the greatest tragedies about the experiences of life is that we don't learn from them. Perhaps the only lesson history teaches is that men don't learn the lesson. I have heard the comment, "Those who don't learn from their mistakes are doomed to repeat them."

Laban remarked to his son-in-law Jacob, "I have learned by experience that the Lord hath blessed me for thy sake" (Gen. 30:27). Experience is a good teacher, and this also applies to the experiences of failure. No failure can ever be judged a loss if a person learns from it. Robert

Schuller wrote, "If my failures teach me something, they will not be without positive value. I can learn from my weaknesses. I can learn something about other people or, if nothing more, I can learn patience, compassion and humility through my failure. This failure may turn out to be the greatest thing that ever happened to me."[4]

Thomas Edison was unsuccessful in the first ninety-six experiments in his attempt to invent the light bulb. An assistant commented to the inventor about this abundance of failure. Mr. Edison answered, "The work is not wasted. We now know ninety-six ways not to do it."

Be Persistent in Conduct

What should you do when you have that failure feeling? What is the proper response to the frustration of failure? Some give up and quit, but you should keep on in the face of failure. Persistence in the experience of failure is the third vital exercise which can result in failure being reversed.

Any significant achievement is the result of making repeated efforts. The line between failure and success is so fine that we can scarcely know when we pass it. That line is so fine that we can be on the line and not know it.

Many people throw up their hands and quit when a little effort or a little more patience would spell success. The prospects for success may seem darkest when really the prospect is changing. A little more persistence may well result in what seems like a hopeless failure becoming a glorious success. Thus, the greater failure would be in no longer trying.

Archie Moore, the boxer, was once asked the key to being a champion. His classic response was, "Fight one more round." Persistence is the name of the game. So if at first you fail, keep on trying.

The early days of World War II were dreary for England. Hitler's armies marched across Europe, achieving victory after victory. The British Expeditionary Force of 200,000 men was trapped in the French seacoast village of Dunkirk in early May, 1940. With their evacuation the only thing that stood between Hitler's seemingly invincible army and the British Isles was a narrow stretch of water called the English Channel. It appeared that England would be invaded and become a part of Hitler's domain.

Winston Churchill, the prime minister, prepared a radio message for the English people in that dark night of impending disaster. In his famous "blood, sweat, and tears" speech he told the English people, "We will never give up." Churchill said, "We shall not flag or fail. We shall go on to the end, we shall fight on the seas and oceans, we shall fight with growing confidence and growing strength in the air, we shall defend our island, whatever the cost may be, we shall fight on the beaches, we shall fight on the landing grounds, we shall fight in the fields and in the streets, we shall fight in the hills; we shall never surrender."[5]

That is the kind of persistence which enables us to reverse life's failures. The people who ultimately win in life are those who never give up.

I once had the privilege of serving as the pastor of a couple who are delightful people. One day they shared thoughts about their marriage. When they were first married, they belonged to different religious faiths which are characterized by strong differences. Some of their friends and family members believed that the marriage would never work.

An added strain was put on the marriage when their firstborn was discovered to be mentally handicapped. By their own admission, they talked about calling it quits. But since so many believed that's what they would do, they decided instead to stick it out "for better or for worse." With renewed determination they worked at making their marriage a success. The result is that they have a union which is not only a source of happiness for them, but which also serves as an excellent example for their friends. What appeared an inevitable failure has turned into a success because of their willingness to persist.

Cloyd M. Chapman described how he found Edison one night in his laboratory. His face was wreathed in smiles. Thinking Edison had solved the problem of the light bulb, Chapman was surprised when Edison commented, "Not a blame thing works. Now I can start over."[6] The fact that our homes, offices, streets, and parks are lighted at night demonstrates that Edison's persistence paid off.

Charles Goodyear conducted countless experiments which were costly and unproductive. His wife begged him to stop before he spent everything they had. He finally yielded to her pleas and for several weeks kept his word. But one day, while his wife was out of the house, he couldn't resist trying again. He was still working on the forbidden experiment when he heard his wife returning. Not wanting her to scold him for going back on his word, Goodyear quickly shoved the mixture into the stove, out of sight.

Hours later, after his wife had left again, he removed

the mixture. To his astonishment, he saw that its appearance had changed. Even more important, the mixture was resistant to heat and cold. Charles Goodyear had stumbled on the process of vulcanization. He did so by his unwillingness to give up.[7]

The persistent spirit which refuses to accept failure as the final, unalterable verdict is what we need in combating the frustration born of temporary failure.

Conclusion

Failure is one of the realities of our experience. It can be the source of some of our worst frustrations in life. It's hard to accept failure and live with the failure feeling. All of us experience this and we recognize the emotional aftermath.

Your greatest failure is to surrender to failure. It is the failure of accepting your failure as final and not trying again or trying something else.

If at first you don't succeed, try, try again.

Notes

1. Maltz, *Psycho-Cybernetics,* p. 125.
2. Maxwell Maltz, *Psycho-Cybernetics and Self-Fulfillment* (New York: Bantam Books, 1978), p. 19.
3. George Weinberg, *Self Creation* (New York: St. Martins Press, 1978), p. 175.
4. Robert H. Schuller, *Self-Love, The Dynamic Force of Success* (Old Tappan, NJ: Spire Books, Fleming H. Revell Co., 1969), p. 133.
5. Winston Churchill, *Heroes of History* (New York: Dodd, Mead & Co., 1968).
6. Harold Blake Walker, *Power to Manage Yourself* (New York: Harper & Brothers, 1955), pp. 73-74.
7. *Tarbell's Teacher's Guide, 1979-80,* Frank S. Mead, Ed. (Old Tappan, NJ: Fleming H. Revell Co., 1979), p. 243.

4

When "I Do" Becomes "I Won't"

The married couple sat in chairs next to each other in my office. Yes, they had a problem in their relationship. They weren't a couple of newlyweds who had suddenly encountered some treacherous rock as they launched out in their new life-relationship. Instead they were seasoned veterans of more than twenty years.

Their problem wasn't due to their leaving the Bible out of their lives or neglecting faith. The man was a deacon. The woman was a Sunday School teacher. Both husband and wife were active in our church, but they still had a problem.

Obviously the fact that they were in my office indicated they knew a problem existed. Previous to their appointment, I had known nothing about the difficulty they were experiencing. The two had suffered for months, but in secret, and now they were ready to share their secret suffering with me.

Their hostility toward each other had reached the point where they wouldn't even talk to one another. Trying to help the couple was not easy. I felt like a communication satellite, receiving their individual signals of complaint and criticism and being asked to relay them. These two were obviously experiencing frustration in marriage.

That couple is one example of millions of people who are experiencing frustration in a relationship which God designed to be one of life's most enjoyable and rewarding. Kay K. Arvin wrote, "Alarm clocks ring every morning to rouse people to begin another day of a discouraged, colorless marriage, or of a vivid, deceitful one."[1] For millions of couples, the "I do" lovingly spoken at the altar, amid the scent of flowers and strains of the wedding march, has become "I won't" spoken with subtle resentment or verbalized hostility.

This smashed dream of young lovers living happily ever after is the source of one of life's most intense frustrations. A woman convert was taking a confirmation examination. "What is matrimony?" the young priest asked her. She answered, "Oh, matrimony is a state of terrible torment which those who enter are compelled to undergo for a time to fit them for heaven." The priest responded, "Oh, no, you've given the definition of purgatory." The elderly bishop interrupted and said, "Maybe she knows more about it than we do."

John Milton's wife was once referred to as a rose. The unhappily married poet heard about the description and responded, "I am no judge of flowers, but it may be so, for I feel the thorns daily." So many couples daily feel the thorns of frustration in marriage. Some have been so deeply pricked that they had rather be dead than wed. A couple went to see a marriage counselor. In seeking to discover some area of common agreement the counselor asked, "Do you have anything in common?" "Yes," answered the wife. "We have one thing in common—neither of us can stand the other."

Recognizably, the situation of frustration in marriage is

complex and multifaceted. There are no simple solutions, but solutions can be found. As we examine this area of frustration, consider the possibility, the problem areas, and the prescription for frustration in marriage.

The Possibility

The possibility of frustration in marriage exists because some couples enter it with unrealistic expectations. George Washington wrote to his granddaughter: "There is no truth more certain than that all our expectations fall short of our enjoyments." This is not always true, but it definitely can be true of marriage if our expectations are unrealistic.

Some couples contemplate marriage with the expectation that their life together will be one of perfect harmony with never a discordant note. Perfect harmony in marriage is an unrealistic expectation. The Gallup Poll reported on the basis of a nationwide survey that four out of five couples readily admitted to having arguments. The pollsters raised their eyebrows about that fifth couple. Perhaps they were like the man who said, "My wife and I never have arguments. However," he continued, "we have had some discussions the neighbors heard a block away."

There are also some couples who enter marriage with the expectation that there will be perpetual glamour. This, too, is an unrealistic expectation. Couples should never become lax in their appearance or consideration of each other. However, marriage becomes daily, and this can tarnish the glamour. My mother-in-law has a plaque in her kitchen which reads, "It begins when she sinks in his arms and ends with her arms in the sink." Moonlight and roses must eventually be blended with daylight and dishwater.

Frustration in marriage is also possible because of difficulties in achieving intimacy. Dr. David Mace defined intimacy in marriage as "shared privacy."[2] The Bible declares that the husband and wife are to be "one flesh" (Gen. 2:24). The "one flesh" concept involves sex, but there is more than sex in the intimacy a couple is to experience.

Achieving a level in the relationship where the two become one without either giving up individuality is not easily done. "The agreement of a man and a woman to become one—to combine their time, energy, money, their dreams, bodies, and personalities into one mutual effort—is entered into with a simple, 'I do.' This is the only simple thing about it."[3]

Without this intimacy, however, the marriage isn't really a marriage. It is only a pretense—a deceitful and shabby imitation of what the Lord designed for a man and woman to experience in the bond of love. Countless couples experience a variety of frustrations in their attempts to achieve this intimacy.

The Problem Areas

I have already acknowledged the fact that the situation of frustration in marriage is complex and multifaceted. Since marriage is an interpersonal relationship, a couple can experience frustration in any area of the relationship. There are, however, some specific areas where problems are likely to be encountered and frustration experienced.

First, *there is the problem of the wrong mate.* It is often stated that "marriages are made in heaven." I agree with that sentiment so long as the subject is marriage as a relationship or institution, and not a reference to each and every marriage. There are some marriages which should never have been contracted. The two persons involved are mismatched.

A domestic court relations judge declared: "Many people today get married who are not fitted or ready, even by modest standards, for marriage. My experience on the bench tells me implicitly that if everyone who applies for a marriage license today were required by law to pass a valid, comprehensive marriage test, half of the applicants would fail and be found presently unsuited for marriage. These are the ones who, in the absence of such a law, I expect to be seeing in my courtroom a few months or years from now."[4] Douglas Watterson wrote, "Marriage counselors constantly face couples who never should have married each other."[5]

There are chemicals and other substances which cannot be mixed. Any attempt to do so is doomed to failure. People are not as inflexible as lifeless matter and therefore are able to adapt and adjust. It is a proven fact, though, that when two people who are not suited for each other get married, and do so for the wrong reasons, their life together will be a frustrating experience.

Second, *there is the problem of poor communication*. Most marriage counselors are agreed that the number-one problem in marriage is poor communication. Ann Landers' credentials and counsel may be questioned by some authorities, but she has been given an inside look into the lives and loves of thousands of people. In many of her columns she has advised, in essence, that communication is the number-one ingredient in a marriage. Most marital problems, she feels, stem from two people not being able to talk with one another. Marriages which last and become truly happy, she observes, are those in which true feelings are expressed—likes, dislikes, means of improvement, and common goals. No matter how tempestuous a marriage is at times, it can survive if there is enough caring to communicate.

Communication is itself a comprehensive subject. There are three general types—verbal, nonverbal, and symbolic. Messages can be sent, missent, and misinterpreted in all three types. The problem in communication can be one's inability to say to one's mate what one really feels, or the inability to understand what that other person is saying back. Real communication takes place only when the receiver has decoded or understood what the messenger is saying.

Added to this problem of understanding is the fact that messages can have double meanings. One young husband returned home from work to find his wife in tears. It was apparent that she had been crying a long time. After his several attempts to get her to say what was wrong, she finally answered, "You called me sugar when you left this morning."

"That's right, honey," the new husband responded. "You're the sweetest person in the world to me."

"No," she replied, "I looked it up in the dictionary and sugar is 'any evaporated sap.' "

Couples can reduce, if not eliminate, frustration in communication if they will follow several essential rules: (1) Plan for time to talk, for communication requires time. One survey revealed that the average couple spent only twenty-six minutes per week in serious conversation. (2) Choose the right time to discuss some subjects. (3) Allow time for evaluation and response. Communication is not a monologue but a dialogue. (4) Be willing to listen.

The Bible says, "Let every man be swift to hear, slow to speak" (Jas. 1:19). Denson Franklin observed that we need more hearing aids and fewer loud speakers.[6] (5) Make sure that what you heard was what was meant. Try saying it back. "What I hear you saying is _____." (6) Do not lose your temper. James added that we are to be "slow to wrath."

Third, *there is the problem area of money management.* Countless couples and families today experience an excessive degree of frustration because of an inflationary economic situation. In many cases inflation has outpaced one's earning power or income. At the same time, people are constantly bombarded with all sorts of commercials and advertisements designed, not only to make the consumer aware of the availability of certain products, but also make them dissatisfied with what they have. The message that comes through is: "The newest is best, and if you don't have it you're out of style." One business author recently estimated that the average American encounters about 2,000 sales messages a day.[7]

The prophet Isaiah asked Hezekiah, "What have they seen in thine house?" (Isa. 39:4). There's usually more in the house than ever before. The pressure to keep up with the Joneses has created its own brand of frustration.

Fourth, *there is the problem area of sexual adjustment.* This area of adjustment in marriage is often the source of much frustration. Marriage counselors recognize that a large number of extramarital affairs are the result of a lack of good sexual adjustment in marriage. Both men and women may seek elsewhere what they don't get at home. Sex is not everything and must never be the sole purpose for marriage. Yet, if it were not for the fact that we are sexual beings there would be no need for marriage.

You cannot build a marriage on sex for "man does not live by bed alone."[8] It takes more than sexual adjustment to make a good marriage, but the lack of adjustment in sexual relations can destroy a marriage. If things aren't right in the master bedroom, they won't be right in the other rooms of the house.

The act of sex is actually the act of marriage. Couples are not to "make love." Instead, they are to give and receive love. This act of marriage, or sexual relations, has a fourfold purpose. (1) Sexual intimacy is an expression of love. (2) The conception of children is a purpose of sex, though children are to be seen as the by-product or the bonus. (3) Sex has the purpose of relieving tension and stress. (4) The sexual relationship is for mutual pleasure and enjoyment.

Since sexual adjustment is a huge area of frustration in a lot of marriages, some suggestions are in order. Husbands and wives should learn about each other. They should be willing to talk about their sexual feelings, their likes and dislikes, and any problems they have. Couples must see sex in its proper relationship. What happens in the bedroom at night is related to what happened at the breakfast table. When a couple goes into their bedroom and closes the door, they don't close out all that has gone before in their relationship that day. Finally, never forget that sex was designed to be an expression of love. To make it anything else—a right to be earned or a reward to be given—is to cheapen both the act and those involved.

The Prescription

More needs to be said as a prescription for the frustration experienced by so many couples. What can be done when the "I do" of commitment has become the "I won't" of conflict?

First, *if frustration experienced in marriage is to be eliminated, the couple must be committed to their marriage.* Frustration in marriage is unavoidable. The possibility of frustration exists because of all marriage is and demands of those involved. This inevitable frustration will win the day unless the two persons involved in the marriage are totally committed to each other. Any practical steps recommended to lessen the tension experienced are inadequate *unless* the two persons are committed to each other and their dream to make their marriage work.

In a counseling session with a couple I suggested some practical steps they could take to resolve some of their tensions. I recognized the merit of my suggestions and made them with the firm belief that their implementation would herald a new day for this couple. Regrettably, the marriage failed and the couple separated. Even though one member of the marriage partnership really wanted to make a go of it, the other did not. It takes two to make a marriage, but only one to destroy it.

These practical steps offered are workable only if there is a commitment on the part of both husband and wife to make their marriage work.

Here is a practical plan which can be used by any couple experiencing frustration in their relationship. Even though the frustration may be the result of tensions or conflicts in any one of a number of areas, these suggestions will help a couple resolve the difficulty and make headway toward the goal of achieving intimacy in marriage.

(1) *Continue to court.* A couple's love grew and developed through courtship. The two often did things which nourished their love. Too often the stresses and strains of

life and family responsibilities can breed a "take-it-for-granted" attitude. Some things in life can be taken for granted, but not people—and never your mate!

A man took his wife to see a psychiatrist. The doctor asked the nature of her problem. The husband responded, "What's-her-name here says I don't pay her enough attention."

In a talk I give to civic clubs, women's meetings, and the like on the theme, "How to Treat Your Mate," I emphasize that there are three things couples should do each day. These are to speak their love (what a message can be conveyed in the three little words, "I love you"); do something special—even if it's a telephone call; and pay a compliment.

(2) *Make time for togetherness.* The demands of daily life can consume time. A man has his work and a woman has hers—whether at home or away. Children take time as do religious, civic, and social responsibilities. If people are not careful, they will find all their waking hours obligated and filled with no time left for "the significant other" in life. Unless couples plan for time together, they won't have any.

I have some friends whose son requires almost constant attention because of brain damage suffered at birth. The couple's time at home is spent caring for this son. Since the man has to make frequent business trips, he arranges to carry his wife sometimes. They make these business trips a time to be together.

(3) *Use tact in expressing grievances.* A couple whose marriage has degenerated to a constant civil war needs to declare a moratorium on criticism. Most of what we crit-

icize in another isn't worth the cost of the criticism. That which should be criticized and corrected could be written down and reserved for a time when the two can sit down and talk calmly. Even then, care must be exercised for the *problem, not the person,* should be attacked.

There are six guidelines to follow in relation to criticism. These are: Can the person tolerate the criticism? Has the criticism been heard before? If it has, the repetition of it could become nagging. Can the person do anything about what you are criticizing? Are you willing to stick around to pick up the pieces? A social worker said, "Criticism is like surgery: It's always painful, and it can be fatal." Are you sure your criticism isn't selfishly motivated? Is criticism what is needed by the person, or is his real need to be encouraged?

In counseling one couple whose relationship had become a constant experience of criticism and recriminations, I recommended the following. First, I suggested that they immediately cease all criticism. Second, those matters which really deserved negative comment were to be written down instead of spoken. However, at the same time each would also write something done by the mate which pleased the other. Third, at an appropriate time these lists containing the negative and positive comments would be shared with each other.

(4) *Pray together.* Couples should not only talk to each other—they should talk to God. And they should do this together. Prayer is no magic wand to be waved and, presto! Everything is made right. However, couples who learn to talk to God together about their problems will not only be availing themselves of his help; they will also be

making strides toward the goal of intimacy.

Conclusion

The "I do" of marriage can become "I won't." This has become the experience of millions. The result is a tremendous amount of frustration. That frustration is either bottled up inside and allowed to sow the seeds of resentment, or it explodes with volcanic fury. The end result is equally disastrous.

We have seen that frustration in marriage is unavoidable. It is inevitable, for marriage is an interpersoanl relationship calling for adjustment and demanding intimacy in many areas. Yet, it is essential that couples learn how to deal with the frustration and the factors which cause it. Try the techniques suggested in this chapter. See if they will work for you and thereby transform the "I won't" of your marriage back to the original "I do."

Notes

1. Kay K. Arvin, *1 + 1 = 1* (Nashville: Broadman Press, 1969), p. 14.

2. David Mace, in an address entitled "Love, Anger, and Intimacy" presented to the Christian Life Commission, "Help for Families," Orlando, Florida, March 28, 1979.

3. Arvin, *1 + 1 = 1*, p. 11.

4. Leland E. Glover, *How to Marry Someone You Can Live with All Your Life* (Englewood Cliffs, NJ: Prentice-Hall, Inc., 1964), p. 1.

5. Douglas Watterson, *Reach Out for Love* (Nashville: Convention Press, 1972), p. 15.

6. Denson N. Franklin, *Faith for Troubled Times* (Westwood, NJ: Fleming H. Revell Company, 1958), p. 59.

7. *Bits And Pieces,* Marvin G. Gregory, Ed. (Fairfield, NJ: Economics Press, Vol. 13, No. 9, September, 1980), p. 24.

8. David Edens, in an address presented to the Christian Life Commission, "Help for Families," Orlando, Florida, March 27, 1979, entitled, "Fulfillment in Marriage."

5

Mountain Climbing Over Molehills

There are days when you think, *If one more thing goes wrong, I'll scream.* I've had my share of such days—and then some. In fact, I had one such day while I was working on this chapter.

It was the day I was to fly to Dallas-Fort Worth to interview a prospective staff member for our church. I drove to the airport and discovered that I had left my wallet in a coat which was hanging in my closet at home. I had some cash in my pocket, but all my credit cards were in that wallet, and I needed one of them to purchase my plane ticket. The airline ticket agent wouldn't take a personal check without some identification, none of which I had because it was in the wallet. I had to go to a bank and get a cashier's check to purchase the plane ticket.

It was pouring rain when I arrived back at the airport right before plane time. Naturally I had to park in a lot some distance from the terminal itself. I tried to get everything I needed in hand before climbing out of the car into the rain and then ran to the terminal, partially protected by my umbrella.

Standing in line at the ticket counter, I realized that the handle of my briefcase felt sticky. Looking down, I discovered that my right hand was smeared with blood. Unknowingly, I had cut a finger in my rush to lock the car. There was blood on my hand, briefcase, and several places on my coat. After buying my ticket, I took the time to treat the cut, wash up, and clean the soiled places on my coat. When I finally came to the gate to board my flight, I found that in the confusion I had misplaced my umbrella!

Finally seated on the plane, I wondered, *What else can go wrong?* But reflecting on the events of the previous hour, I realized that each of the above-described happenings wasn't a major, earth-shattering tragedy. Not a single one of them, nor all of them combined, had kept me from doing what I had set out to do that day. Furthermore, each one of these "great mountains of trouble" had been easily overcome. Thinking about it, I discovered that I had been on the verge of mountain climbing over molehills.

Life has its daily annoyances and little frustrating trifles. These are just that—little things and not major tragedies. But they can so easily become the straw that breaks the camel's back. In the words of Solomon, they can become the little foxes that spoil the tender vines of a day.

One of the characters in George Santayana's novel, *The Last Puritan*, remarks: "Ah, the little troubles, Mr. Oliver, they ruin a woman's life." They can also ruin a man's life. A day for you may begin bright and sunny with promise. But before you know it a string of little trifles has rushed onto the stage of the day, stealing the show. The initial optimism and elation with which you faced the day is soon replaced with a brooding pessimism as you wonder, *What will go wrong next?* If you stopped to look more closely you'd see that no major tragedy has cast a cloud of doom over your head. Instead, your feeling of frustration is the end result of many little pests—just molehills you have made into mountains.

A tire on the car is flat, or maybe the car won't start because of a loose battery cable. One of the children knocks over a glass of milk. The traffic is a little slower than usual, or you get behind someone in the check-out lane who can't find enough change. It's raining when you leave the beauty parlor, or the barber cut your hair a trifle shorter than you like. Junior got mud on the clean jeans you'd just put on him, or Dad is a few minutes late for supper. Now really, are any one of these big deals? Yet if we aren't careful, they'll darken our moods.

Many of us are guilty of mountain climbing over molehills such as these. We make these little annoyances more than they actually are. In so doing we create some bad situations for ourselves and those around us. It's an extreme example of what I mean, but several years ago I read about a shooting which left one man dead and another in jail on a charge of murder. The argument which led to the shooting and death was over one cigarette! Talk about mountain climbing over molehills! However, our own experiences prove that many of the little annoyances have caused us to react in such an extreme manner that we have created a bad situation for us and others.

In learning to handle the frustrations of life, we need to learn how to keep from mountain climbing over molehills. So much of the frustration we experience is a matter of a dollar's worth of adrenaline expended over a dime's worth of aggravation. We could save ourselves all kinds of anxiety if only we could learn to recognize that a molehill is not a mountain.

How can we keep from mountain climbing over the molehills of life? This we must do, because more times than not, it's these little things that do us in. I offer two general suggestions.

Practice Restraint

When the little annoyances or trifles of life pop up, our initial frustration-inclination is to complain or kick. Columnist Robert C. Ruark, for example, was annoyed by pigeons. He felt that the whole pigeon tribe was arrogant, offensive, and good for nothing. He expressed his annoyance with pigeons by kicking one. He didn't find it a satisfying experience, but concluded, "There are so many elusive annoyances that need a boot in the tail, and the opportunity occurs too seldom."

Ruark discovered that kicking pigeons doesn't make them go away, and neither does kicking the little annoyances that cause us frustration. What the kicking can do, though, is create a worse situation. All of us can think of personal experiences which got out of hand because somebody kicked. The kick may have given momentary satisfaction, but the consequences that came were not exactly what we wanted. Reflecting on the situation later, we found ourselves wishing we had practiced a little restraint.

John Sutherland Bonnell reminds us that, "Life is not an easy matter for any of us. It demands self-mastery. . . . We must discipline our emotions."[1] Some of that discipline is learning how and when to "cool it."

I believe this is particularly true when the petty annoyances of life involve another person. We can get ourselves into some unwanted predicaments if we impulsively and irrationally respond to the person-caused annoyance by kicking or speaking out.

One day I came out of a hospital where I had been visiting to find a woman half-leaning, half-sitting on the front fender of my automobile. Those who know me well realize that I have love affairs with my automobiles and become upset when someone "hurts" one of my "loves." Because I have occasionally spoken out when I discovered someone doing what that woman was doing, I was ready to talk with her about her unwarranted liberty with my car.

But something made me feel I should practice restraint and hold my tongue. How thankful I am that I did! When I came next to the woman I saw the unmistakable burns from cobalt treatment on her neck and realized that she was feeling sick from a dose just administered. If I had responded to my initial annoyance by speaking out, and then had seen her predicament, I would have ended up feeling so small I would have given an insect a superiority complex.

The anonymous author of a jingle speaks truth about dealing with people who annoy us:

> There's a fellow in your office
> Who complains and carps and whines
> Till you'd almost do a favor
> To his heirs and his assigns!
> But I'll tip you to a secret,
> And this queer chap is involved—
> He's no enemy to fight with,
> He's a problem to be solved.

We are usually inclined to kick and gripe when the trifles of life wander onto the stage of a day, upsetting us by their unwanted presence. But things will be better for us and others if we learn to practice restraint by exercising patience and understanding.

Practice Recognition

First, *recognize that the upsetting trifles of molehills are a part of life.* Of course, in some cases we can do something to eliminate them. How often we become upset over some little thing a family member or a friend does, and that person isn't even aware that the action annoys us. A simple request or suggestion made in the right spirit and tone of voice can easily eliminate many little annoyances around our homes and places of work.

On the other hand, little annoyances are part of the fabric of life and none of us can fully escape them. We must learn to accept these trifles as inescapable bits of sand that sift into the machinery of day-to-day living. Harold Walker wrote: "There is no use being stubborn about things you cannot change. The result is simply permanent frustration."[2]

Second, *in recognizing that little frustrating events are a part of life, look for the humor in them.* It is hard to laugh at times, but it might be better for us than crying. A little boy fell off his tricycle and to the surprise of his mother, he began to laugh. When she asked him why, the little fellow responded, "I'm laughing so I won't cry."

When Jacob sent his sons into Egypt to seek help during a famine, he instructed them to "take . . . a little honey" (Gen. 43:11). The journey of life will also be much more pleasant for us and those traveling with us if we take a little honey with us—a little humor to sweeten the sour moments of living.

After shopping, a young preacher's wife returned home with a new dress. Since the couple was living on a very limited income, the purchase of the dress had completely destroyed their budget. In spite of his holy calling, the husband responded in a typical husbandly manner—he hit the ceiling! "Why did you do it?" he thundered.

His young wife explained that she saw the dress in a store window and felt there would be no harm in trying it on.

"But why did you buy it?" he barked.

"Well," she answered with a twinkle in her eye, "I guess the devil tempted me."

In a solemn, sermonic voice the husband asked, "But why didn't you say, 'Get thee behind me, Satan'?"

The young wife answered, "I did, and he said, 'The dress looks good from the back, too.'"

The wife's humor had the effect of defusing the tension of frustration. Sometimes it will take a lot of looking, but we too will be helped in handling the little annoyances of life if we look for humor in them.

Third, *in the practice of recognition see that these trifles are just that—trifles*. If we look at them too closely, we will blow them up out of all proportion. A dime is a very small coin, but if it's held right before your eye it can blot out everything else. If we look only at the trifles and nothing else, they will seem as mountains when they're only molehills.

Screwtape, in C. S. Lewis' book, *The Screwtape Letters* is an undersecretary of Satan charged with the task of supervising a man until he arrives in hell at the end of his days on earth. Each time this demonic assistant gets in

trouble, he writes a letter to Satan seeking advice. On one
occasion the demon is in trouble because his human has
joined a church.

He writes a letter to the underworld asking what to do.
Satan replies that the matter is not as serious as it seems.
He counsels his emissary to be sure to stay with his man at
all times, especially in church. Then Satan advises him,
"Keep him aware of little things"—of the fact that the
usher is a hypocrite, that his shoes squeak, that the lady's
hat doesn't fit properly. Satan says never "Let him see the
church with her banners flying for that is a sight at which
all hell trembles."[3]

When the little things that annoy and frustrate begin to
pile up on the stage of a day, back off for a moment and
see the big things. Then you'll be able to gauge everything
in its proper perspective. Charles Allen related an experience he once had:

> In Panama City, Florida, for a week's revival, I had a
> hotel room overlooking the great Gulf of Mexico. It was a
> stimulating experience, and while there I thought of a great
> prescription that a very wise physician gave a patient. He
> told him to "get off and look at something big."[4]

This is good advice that's frequently stressed in the
Bible. The Lord advises, "Be still, and know that I am
God" (Ps. 46:10). The psalmist sang, "I will lift up mine
eyes unto the hills, from whence cometh my help" Ps.
121:1). The ancient prophet spoke to his people, "Get thee
up into the high mountain" and "Behold your God!"
(Isa. 40:9). When things seem to be going wrong on every
hand, we need to do as Daniel and remember, "There is a
God in heaven" (Dan. 2:28).

Conclusion

Each day many of us waste the precious energy of life and literally wear ourselves out by mountain climbing over molehills. The molehills are in our paths daily, and most of them can't be evaded. They pose no real obstacles to us in the pilgrimage of life, but we're frequently guilty of making them as big as mountains.

The molehills are just little things—they're only little annoyances and the causes of frustration in life. But if we're not careful, they will easily become "the foxes, the little foxes, that spoil the vines" (Song of Sol. 2:15). To keep this from happening, practice restraint and recognition.

Notes

1. John Sutherland Bonnell, *No Escape from Life* (New York: Harper Chapel Books, Harper & Row, Publishers, 1958), p. 185.

2. Walker, *Power to Manage Yourself,* p. 107.

3. C. S. Lewis, *The Screwtape Letters* (New York: The Macmillan Company, 1944).

4. Charles L. Allen, *In Quest of God's Power* (Westwood, NJ: Fleming H. Revell Company, 1952), p. 61.

6

Beware of the Short Fuse

During the post-season bowl games of 1978, millions of Americans watching television beheld a demonstration of the danger of having a short fuse. Woody Hayes, highly successful football coach at Ohio State University, had the reputation of having a short fuse and was known for his anger-antics during ball games. He frequently provided a show for the spectators with his outburst of anger. But "the straw that broke the camel's back" came in the Gator Bowl game in 1978. Hayes became angry one time too many.

Ohio State was playing Clemson University. The Buckeyes were behind, but were driving for a possible touchdown when Clemson's middle guard, Charlie Bauman, intercepted an Ohio State pass to seal the victory for the South Carolina team. Bauman was driven out of bounds on the Ohio State side of the field. Coach Hayes, in a fit of anger, slugged the Clemson player. The next week the Ohio State Board of Regents relieved the controversial coach of his job.

Even though most of us were shocked by what we saw, and agree that such conduct is unbecoming a coach who is supposed to set an example for others, we cannot help but sympathize with Hayes. After all, who of us has not allowed anger to get the best of us in some situation? Like the well-known coach, all of us have needed, or now need, help in dealing with anger.

Anger is definitely related to the experiences of frustration. Charles F. Kemp wrote that "Anger is usually the result of frustration with a person or situation." When things don't happen the way we want them to and our needs are unmet, we often express the resulting frustration in angry outbursts or with a slow burn. In some cases, the fuse of anger is so short that it doesn't take much of a spark to ignite it. If you program yourself to be offended whenever you don't get your way, you could be angry nearly always. So, we need to beware of the short fuse of anger in facing and handling the frustrations of life.

In dealing with the short fuse of anger, we need to understand the problem with anger, the propriety of anger, and the prescription for anger.

The Problem with Anger

The first thing we need to clearly establish about frustration anger is that anger is real. One of our difficulties in dealing with the emotion of anger is that we frequently attempt to deny its reality. It's so easy for us to call what we are feeling by another name. I don't suppose there is any emotion that is called by as many different names as anger. The following is certainly not a comprehensive list, but it does depict our attempt to deny the reality of anger by calling it something else:

> Antagonism, annoyance, and aggravation; bitterness; crossness; defiance and displeasure; exasperation and excitement; being fed up; frustration, and ferocity; being griped; hostility and hurt; indignance, irritation, being

infuriated, and being irked; being mad; being offended and outraged; provocation and peevishness; rage and resentment; being sore and seething; and being upset.

How many times we respond to the question, "Are you angry?" by answering with one of these words. The very answer is an attempt to deny the reality of anger and refuse to face the truth that we are indeed angry.

Whether or not we are willing to admit it, anger is a real problem for many of us, and our expressions of it cause us even more problems. Like Woody Hayes, we too have suffered some loss as a result of our inability to handle anger in general and frustration anger in particular. Even when the anger is justified, or a proper emotional response to a life situation, the incorrect expression of it has at times created problems for us.

The Bible addresses the problem of anger and the wrong expressions of it. Consider this potpourri of biblical statements about the short fuse of anger:

> Refrain from anger and forsake wrath! Fret not yourself; it tends only to evil.

> A man of quick temper acts foolishly.

> He who is slow to anger has great understanding, but he who has a hasty temper exalts folly.

> A soft answer turns away wrath, but harsh words stir up anger.

> A hot-tempered man stirs up strife, but he who is slow to anger quiets contention.

> He who is slow to anger is better than the mighty, and he who rules his spirit than he who takes a city.

> Good sense makes a man slow to anger, and it is his glory to overlook an offense.
>
> Make no friendship with a man given to anger, nor go with a wrathful man, lest you learn his ways and entangle yourself in a snare.
>
> Wrath is cruel, anger is overwhelming.
>
> For pressing milk produces curds, pressing the nose produces blood, and pressing anger produces strife (Ps. 37:8; Prov. 14:17,29; 15:1,18; 16:32; 19:11; 22:24-25; 27:4; and 30:33, RSV).

Added to these biblical admonitions and observations about anger are the words of Paul to put away anger, wrath, and malice (Col. 3:8), and not to let the sun go down on your wrath (Eph. 4:26). David Edens paraphrased Paul by saying, "Simmer down before sundown."

Anger, therefore, is a fact of our nature—a fact that poses a problem. Anger has resulted in ample misery for us and those whose lives we touch. Quite frequently we feel the flush of this emotion as a result of some experience of frustration. Even though it may range from a mild displeasure to blind rage, anger is often a part of the agony of frustration.

The Propriety of Anger

Since anger is a reality of life, is it ever justified? Or is anger always a sin—a roaring beast in the zoo of the untamed human nature? In response to these questions, let me quickly note that many students of human behavior recognize the propriety of anger. Dr. James Mallory wrote: "Anger is by no means an evil in itself. It's one of the most important emotions we can have because of the motivation it gives to us."[1]

The question of propriety cannot be that easily dismissed, however. Even though anger is fundamental to human nature and a natural response to injury, that doesn't legitimize all anger or give us a license to express it as we choose. The fact of the matter is that anger involves more than a natural response to injury—it also involves choice.

Some people go so far as to suggest that we can actually program ourselves not to become angry at all. Wayne Dyer wrote that "Anger is a choice, as well as a habit. It is a learned reaction to frustration in which you behave in ways that you would rather not."[2] He added, "Anger, that hurtful emotional response to obstacles, can be eliminated.[3] The practitioners of Transactional Analysis (TA) and Rational Emotive Therapy (RET) stress that one can control one's anger by controlling one's thoughts. In TA it is pointed out that anger is usually the expression of the rebellious child-ego state. RET contends that all feelings, including anger, are the result of the thoughts preceding them. These are called internal sentences. If a person's internal sentences are of frustration and anger, then one's feelings will be angry feelings. Dyer explains and expounds:

> Like all emotions, anger is the result of thinking. It is not something that simply happens to you. When faced with circumstances that are not going the way you would like them to, you tell yourself that things shouldn't be that way

(frustration) and then you select a familiar angry response which serves the purpose.[4]

Many of us, though, are aware that anger involves more than merely the mental predisposition of getting mad whenever something or someone doesn't agree with us. David Mace said, "Despite the teaching of some modern cults, we do not make ourselves angry, and are not responsible for being in a state of anger."[5]

I have personally been helped in my own battle by understanding the anatomy of anger itself. First, exactly what is anger? It has been defined as a strong emotion of displeasure and a natural, reflective result of frustration— our reaction to having a goal blocked. Dr. Mace wrote: "Anger is a spontaneous response to a situation in which my sense of security is threatened, my self-esteem is damaged, my feelings hurt."[6]

Second, what happens when a person becomes angry? From a physiological standpoint, anger is the body's way of responding to danger. That response is spontaneous and automatic. Dr. Mace observed anger is "A complex series of body changes triggered off by a sudden awareness of danger."[7]

When you become angry, a series of changes automatically take place in the body. The heart begins to beat faster. The blood pressure goes up, and the flow of blood is redirected. Instead of going into the organs of the body, the blood flows into the muscles, causing them to tense. Anticoagulants are removed from the bloodstream and an adrenaline-like substance flows into the blood, giving the body a new burst of energy. All of this is to the end that the person is equipped for one of two things—flight or fight.

Third, the decision of what we do with all this energy is up to us. The body is prepared for a fight or flight. We decide which it will be.

This leads to the obvious conclusion that the impropriety in anger is not in being angry but in how we handle it. We can't keep from becoming angry. This is a natural, God-given response to a threat, whether real, anticipated, or imagined. How we respond to that threat and handle the body power of anger is up to us. Tragically, our experience is that we usually respond wrongfully.

People usually respond to anger in one of three ways. Even though a person may be characterized by one of the three more than the other two, all three responses to anger are made from time to time.

For example, the man who usually manifests anger by blowing up and freely venting it like an exploding volcano, will suppress his anger when it is directed toward his boss or a policeman who is giving him a ticket for a traffic violation. He does so because he knows the consequences that could come from acting in his usual explosive manner. On the other hand, the individual who usually keeps his anger to himself will occasionally reach a point where he has taken all he can and he explodes.

The fact that our anger is not always expressed the same way in every situation was illustrated by a young woman with whom I talked. Since I was to speak on anger at a couples' retreat that evening, I asked her how she expressed her anger. She replied that when she became angry at a friend she usually went off by herself for awhile, but when she became angry at her brother she yelled at him. It is obvious that her responses to anger were dictated by the circumstances.

The first general response to anger is to *repress it*. This is simply refusing to face the fact that you are angry. H. Norman Wright wrote: "Repression of anger is the worst possible response that we can make to being angry. Unfortunately, it is an all too common response among Christians."[8]

Some Christians, who have been taught that being angry is a sin, deal with their anger-feelings by denying them. As already noted, they call the anger by another name which to them lessens the reality of it. But repressed anger will eventually rear its head in the form of tension, depression, and psychosomatic disorders such as headaches, high blood pressure, stomach problems, and a variety of mysterious pains. Dr. Mallory wrote that the energy and tension of anger, "If not dissipated, works destructively in our bodies."[9] John Powell noted, "When I repress my emotions, my stomach keeps score."[10]

The second general response to anger is to *suppress it*. To suppress anger is to put the lid on it. You recognize that you are angry, but you try to keep your anger under control instead of letting it loose. Proverbs 14:29 says, "A wise man controls his temper. He knows that anger causes mistakes" (TLB). As we have seen, this is a proper response in some situations.

However, this can also be a dangerous response if the lid is kept on permanently. By suppressing anger you can avoid the unwanted consequences that can come from a free expression of it, but at the same time you face the real possibility of dire consequences for yourself. As already stated, anger results in physiological changes. Putting the lid on anger doesn't automatically reverse these changes. The fire within may not be set free, but that doesn't mean that it automatically goes out. Suppressing anger without ever releasing it is like storing TNT in your basement. Eventually there will be an explosion.

The third general response to anger is to *express it*. People often lose their tempers and fly off the handle. They flail away at the cause of the anger. This expression is usually verbal and sometimes violent. The consequences of such expressions, particularly in the area of interpersonal relationships, is costly.

The news reports frequently contain items about abused wives and children. In fact, it is estimated that one half of the wives in America have been physically abused by their husbands—usually in a fit of anger. Police answer some ten million calls each year in response to domestic fights, and the statisticians claim that for every domestic altercation reported to the police there are five that go unreported.

Of course, there are some therapeutic ways to express anger. We can learn to redirect our anger. One woman, when asked how she expressed her hostility toward her husband, answered, "Well, when he leaves in the morning, I swish his toothbrush in the toilet bowl."[11] Some people learn to work anger out in physical exercise or some activity demanding physical exertion. Another woman stated that when she got mad, she took all the rugs out of her house and beat them. She added that she had the cleanest rugs in town! This demonstrates that getting angry and expressing it doesn't have to mean losing control of yourself or making yourself miserable.

The Prescription for Anger

Anger is a normal and natural emotion generated by frustration. Since some ways of responding to it have disastrous consequences, how can we deal with our anger without destroying us or others in the process? We have seen the impropriety involved in responding to our anger by repressing, suppressing, and expressing it.

Beyond question the wisest response is to *confess it*. This is the healthiest and least destructive way of dealing with our anger. This is true because three events may take place in the confession of anger. First, the person confessing admits that he has a problem. Second, the confession makes it possible to determine whether the occasion for anger is real or imagined—and therefore unjustified. Third, the confession of anger made properly shares the responsibility for resolving the anger with other people.

This is vitally essential in dealing with anger within marriage and the family. Even though only one person is angry, others in the home are definitely involved. They have a responsibility to help resolve the anger and the situation which prompted it.

In the confession of anger, a person is not attacking the cause, but honestly admitting a condition. Expressing anger usually involves *aggression* while the confession of anger is an *admission*. Expressing anger is usually an impulsive act resulting in irrational behavior and injurious words. Confessing anger is a deliberate choice made with a restraining control on one's emotions.

Since anger remains until it is redirected or is resolved, the prescription of confession is to be administered as quickly as possible. This was the meaning of Paul's statement, "Do not let the sun go down on your anger" (Eph. 4:26, RSV). The King James version calls it "wrath" in this verse. Anger is to be handled on a daily basis. Each new day will have a dark cloud if one enters it encumbered with the smelly garbage of yesterday's anger. Dealing with anger as soon as possible is the only way to keep it from growing and spreading like a poison throughout the entirety of one's life, developing into deep-seated resentment and bitterness. William Blake wrote:

> I was angry with my friend:
> I told my wrath, my wrath did end.
> I was angry with my foe:
> I told him not, my wrath did grow.

A final word about the prescription for anger: Seek to learn from experience. Anger can be a source of growth if it is handled properly. Doctors Frank Minirth and Paul Meier wrote: "Verbalizing our anger tactfully produces intimacy in a marriage or in a friendship."[12] Writing about conflict in marriage, Dwight Small pointed out the good that can come from the right handling of anger: "As a reality in marriage, conflict can be creatively managed for good; it is part of the growth process. Don't ever underestimate its positive possibilities! . . . In Christian marriage, conflict—with its demands for confession, forgiveness, and reconciliation—is a means God employs to teach humility."[13]

Conclusion

Anger is one of the most difficult emotions to handle. Remember, you can't keep from becoming angry. Anger is a natural response to provocation. However, even though you can't keep from becoming angry, you can choose how you'll handle it. When you realize you are angry, you have a split second in which to decide how you will respond.

Failing to choose is in itself a decision. The one who doesn't consciously use that split second to make a response decision will usually respond in the manner commensurate with one's nature. If one is shy and retiring, one will most likely suppress or repress one's anger. If one is outgoing and vocal, one will probably explode all over the countryside.

If we use that split second, between the realization that we are angry and the response to the anger, to look at the situation and then decide, we can make anger work for us. In that fraction of time we can determine if the cause of anger is worth a response and decide to redirect the anger energy if it isn't.

Or we can determine that a response is needed and at the same time select the best one. It may be we'll see that the time is not right for a response or that we aren't fully in control of our feelings, and then decide to wait until later. But we'll have accepted responsibility for our anger response and can use our anger rather than be used by it. In so doing, we'll be spared the danger of the short fuse.

Notes

1. James D. Mallory, *The Kink and I* (Wheaton, IL: Victor Books, 1975), p. 185.

2. Wayne W. Dyer, *Your Erroneous Zones* (New York: Funk & Wagnalls, 1976), p. 210.

3. Ibid., p. 211.

4. Ibid., p. 210.

5. David Mace, in an address entitled, "Love, Anger, and Intimacy" presented to the Christian Life Commission, "Help for Families," Orlando, Florida, March 28, 1979.

6. Ibid.

7. Ibid.

8. H. Norman Wright, *Communication: Key to Your Marriage* (Glendale: Regal Book Division, G. L. Publications, 1978), p. 91.

9. Mallory, *The Kink and I,* p. 177.

10. John Powell, *Why Am I Afraid to Tell You Who I Am?* (Argus Communications, 1969), p. 155.

11. David Edens, in an address presented to the Christian Life Commission, "Help for Families," Orlando, Florida, March 27, 1979, entitled, "Fulfillment in Marriage."

12. Frank B. Minirth and Paul D. Meier, *Happiness Is a Choice* (Grand Rapids: Baker Book House, 1978), p. 154.

13. Dwight Hervey Small, *After You've Said I Do* (Old Tappan, NJ: Spire Books, Fleming H. Revell, 1968, 1978), pp. 159, 178.

7

When Life Doesn't Give You
a Second Chance

The chaplain in George Bernard Shaw's play, *St. Joan,* was gripped with regret. He consented to the death of Joan and witnessed her execution as she was burned at the stake. Later he cried out in anguish:

> You don't know: you haven't seen: it is so easy to talk when you don't know. . . . But when it is brought home to you; when you see the thing you have done; when it is blinding your eyes, stifling your nostrils, tearing your heart, then—then—O God, take away this sight from me! O Christ, deliver me from this fire that is consuming me! She cried to Thee in the midst of it: Jesus! Jesus! Jesus! She is in Thy bosom; and I am in hell forevermore.[1]

The chaplain felt the awesomeness of regret. I once conducted the funeral service for a woman I didn't know. Her daughter was a member of my congregation. After the funeral, the daughter came to me, burdened by failure. Her mother was not a professing Christian and died without making any life commitment to Christ, so far as the family knew. The daughter stated that, even though she herself was a Christian, she had never talked to her mother about Christ. Her failure to follow through when she had the opportunities had been eased by the promise to herself that one day she would witness to her mother. Suddenly her mother was stricken with a heart attack and died. In her grief the daughter lamented that she would no longer have opportunities to talk with her mother about the most important matter of all. Her failure had become permanent and unalterable. Life would give her no second chance to witness to her mother. The daughter was consumed with regret.

In chapter 3 I examined failure and its being a common experience for everyone. I emphasized that there is frustration in failure. This was labeled failure frustration. Optimistically, we also recognized that failure doesn't have to be final. When we keep on in the face of failure, we can turn some failures into victories.

Yet, there are times when life doesn't give us a second chance. The chaplain in *St. Joan* could never have a second chance to side with the young woman he helped burn at the stake. The young woman who sought my counsel would never have another opportunity to talk with her mother about Christ. There are occasions when once-in-a-lifetime opportunities come to us. When we fail to make the most of them, they are forever gone.

In those situations where we have no second chance, the frustration of failure is compounded by the emotion of regret and remorse. Regret is a universal experience. It is sorrow for what has happened. "It is," as Roger Crook writes, "merely a look at the past with sorrow."[2] Regret thus becomes one of the many faces of frustration. We are sorry we didn't do what we should have done when we had the chance and now wish we had the opportunity to do it.

To be certain, regret doesn't always have moral or spiritual implications. We may feel regret because of some decision or action which was not morally wrong or spiritually injurious. We may even sense regret over the misdeeds of others, even though we had no part in them, or even the opportunity to do anything about their errors. The worst type of regret, though, comes from our failure to make the most of an opportunity. This experience of regret is further intensified when we realize that we won't ever have another opportunity in which to act differently regarding our failure. So, regret is related to frustration.

What are we to do when life doesn't give us a second chance? I honestly don't remember my words to the young woman who sought my counsel. But if she were sitting in my office now, I would advise her to release the past, reserve self-judgment, and receive God's forgiveness. I quickly add that these are interrelated steps for dealing with regret. Each must be exercised, and even though I treat them separately, in a sense they are three parts of a whole.

Release the Past

In a "Peanuts" cartoon by Charles Schulz, Lucy is seen open for business at her psychiatric help booth. Of course, her patient is Charlie Brown. Lucy gives her opinion about life: "Charlie Brown, life is like sitting in a deck chair." When he asks what she means by that, Lucy continues, "You know that people on an ocean liner sit in deck chairs. Some sit at the front of the ship to see where they're going, and some sit at the back of the ship looking at where they've been."

When she askes where he's sitting, Charlie Brown answers, "I can't even get my deck chair open." At times we may feel like Charlie Brown, completely out of it. However, there are many people looking at life in terms of where they've been. They have an inordinate attachment to the past.

So many people moan, "If only I hadn't done that! If only I hadn't said that! If only I could do it over again." This is doing what the Transactional Analysts call playing the game, "If only."

When he was young, Arthur Gordon was bogged down in the consequence of several bad decisions he had made in the recent past. He sought help from a counselor. After listening to him for a while, the counselor said: "The refrain I hear you repeating over and over again is summed up in two words: 'if only' this or 'if only' that. You are eating yourself up with remorse and recrimination. Let me make a suggestion. Substitute two other words for 'if only,' namely, 'next time.' That will get you to focusing on the part of life where something can be done. There is nothing you can do about the past except learn from it and resolve to make the future different because of it. That is what the words 'next time' will do. They get you out of the quagmire of remorse and get you to dealing with the only creative thing left—the present and the future."[3]

The fact is, once something is done, it's done. Once something is said, it's said. It's not within the power of anyone to turn back the hands of the clock and thus relive a moment now past in order that we might do differently. Omar Khayyam wrote in *The Rubáiyát:*

> The Moving finger writes,
> and having writ,
> Moves on: nor all your

> Piety nor Wit shall lure it back to
> Cancel out half a Line;
> Nor all your tears wash
> out a single Word of it.[4]

The past cannot be changed. It is forever set. That truth should stand as a warning signal before our minds every day of our lives, reminding us to live as we should each day.

Since the past is past, it is necessary for us to release our hold on it. The person who tries to hold onto yesterday will discover that it becomes a millstone around his neck. The practice of holding onto the past can result in the ruin of life. Hugh Walpole in his book, *Hans Frost,* has a character who remarks about some people, "They slap the face of the present with the dead hand of the past."

One of the characters in Margaret Mitchell's *Gone with the Wind,* says, "The world cannot beat us. But we can lick ourselves by longing for the things we don't have anymore, and by remembering too much." There is wisdom in these words.

One day William Gladstone was out walking with a friend. They passed through a pasture gate, and the friend, who went through the gate last, neglected to close it. Gladstone turned and closed the gate. He remarked: "I have made it a habit all through life to close gates behind me." The gate of the past is one we need to close, locking behind us the events of yesterday.

The more we try to hold onto yesterday, continually reliving the events of the past in memory, the greater becomes our sense of regret. Even though the deed is not repeatedly done, by our continually rehearsing the past the grief and regret born of our failure is kept fresh daily. It is only by releasing the past—that is already gone anyway—that healing can begin and the grip of regret can be broken.

Reserve Your Judgment

When we face the fact of our failures, mistakes, and shortcomings, we tend toward one of two extremes. On the one hand, people try to ignore their failure and explain away their guilt. On the other hand, there are some who are guilty of overly condemning themselves. It is easy for us in the face of our failures to gravitate to one of these two extremes. Both of them are wrong.

Jesus Christ presented a story about two men whose words expressed these two extremes (Luke 18:9-14). One of the men in the story was a Pharisee. He went to the Temple to pray and in his prayer extolled his virtues, while admitting no vices. To be sure, he was certainly guilty of sins. But the Pharisee confessed no sins for he felt he had none to confess.

The other character in Jesus' story was a publican. His very identification cried out, "Sinner." The publican didn't seek to conceal this fact, but readily admitted it in his confession. In his prayer he implored, "God be merciful to me *the* sinner" [author's italics]. Even though our translations have the article "a" rather than "the," the Greek text reads "the sinner." The publican was so convicted of his own sins that he saw himself as the only sinner in the world. For a fact, he was a sinner, but he wasn't the only sinner in the world. His self-judgment, though correct, was too exclusive.

When we are in the grip of regret, we tend to do as the

publican did. We tend to judge ourselves too harshly. We can be so conscious of our failures or sins that we forget about any good we've done. All of us are an unusual mixture of good and bad. This is a part of the mystery of every person—no one of us is totally good, but neither are we totally bad. However, in our act of self-judgment, we can so focus on the wrong done that we forget everything else. We tend to see only the error we've committed and not the excellence in other areas of life.

It's wrong for a person to feel he has done no wrong, especially when that wrong is so apparent. But it's also wrong for a person to feel that he's all wrong. Such a low opinion of self has led some to say, "Because of what I've done, everything about me is worthless and I'm worthless."

This unbalanced self-judgment can easily have dreadful results. Seeing only the mistake—and nothing else, plus blowing the failure out of proportion—can lead a person to such despair that he actually does physical harm to himself.

Judas Iscariot is a biblical example of the consequence of an overly harsh self-judgment. Whatever his reason for betraying Jesus, when Judas saw what the Jewish authorities intended to do with Christ, he sought to undo what he had done. It was too late for that—the deed was irrevocably done. Thus filled with remorse, Judas went out and hanged himself.

Depression is one of the leading causes of suicide, and one facet of depression is a sense of remorse or regret because of failure. Authorities state that suicide is the tenth leading cause of death in the United States, accounting for twenty-four thousand deaths a year. Added to this

is the fact that there are an estimated ten unsuccessful suicide attempts for every successful one.[5] Every three minutes someone attempts suicide, and every twenty minutes
someone succeeds.[6]

Frank Minirth and Paul Meier quoted authorities who
have identified ten warning signs of individuals most likely
to attempt suicide.[7] Five of these ten signs relate to experiences of regret and remorse born of some failure in life.
These five are:

1. Individuals with intense emotional pain, as seen in
   depression.
2. Individuals with intense hopeless feelings.
3. Individuals who have experienced a significant loss of
   some kind.
4. Individuals with an intense need to achieve.
5. Individuals with an excess of disturbing life events
   within the last six months.

Doctors Minirth and Meier added, "Most people who
commit suicide do so when they are not seeing things real-
istically. They would not commit suicide if they saw the
true nature of the situation and realized their problem was
only temporary and solvable."[8] This truth underscores the
fact that self-judgment must be reserved for a later time.

Paul told the Corinthian church that he didn't judge
himself (1 Cor. 4:3). He meant that the final judgment of
his deeds and service was to be reserved until God would
do it. The apostle was aware that God knew things about
his (Paul's) life that he didn't know and that God's judgment would be both complete and fair.

The apostle's conviction is good advice for us when we
are gripped by regret. Our self-judgment can be much too

severe, and that is as wrong as the Pharisee in absolving ourselves of all guilt.

Receive God's Forgiveness

It isn't enough in dealing with regret and remorse to close the door on yesterday and reserve self-judgment. As important as these two steps are, they do nothing about the sense of guilt we experience as a result of our failures.

Guilt is defined as "Feelings of culpability arising from behavior or desires contrary to one's ethical principles."[9] It is the feeling we have when we act contrary to what we've been taught to do or feel we ought to do. Guilt is a definite facet of the experience of regret.

Meursault is one of the characters in Albert Camus's *The Stranger*. The crime for which he was ultimately convicted was the absence of any guilt at all. This isn't true of us. Like the chaplain in Shaw's play, we often feel the consuming fire of guilt. Like the young woman who failed to talk to her mother about God, we usually feel guilty over our failures.

To be sure, some guilt may be neurotic—or without any real justification—but that doesn't make it any less real to the person. Furthermore, guilt unresolved can do tremendous harm to the person. A leading psychiatrist said: "Most of the cases of mental derangement of a functional type are due to a sense of guilt." Harold Walker reminds us that "Guilt devastates the kingdom of the mind and of the emotions until we hate ourselves."[10] We see that something must be done about the guilt factor in our regret.

There are only two options available when we accept the fact of our guilt. These are to either punish ourselves or to seek forgiveness. Cecil Osborne wrote that "Man is so constituted that his guilt must be either fully forgiven or he will find ways, by an inexorable inner mechanism, to punish himself."[11] He added, "We punish ourselves quite as inexorably for false guilt as for real guilt."[12]

Sigmund Freud pointed out that many people deliberately commit some wrong act because it is certain to bring punishment. That punishment will, they believe, alleviate the sense of guilt they have because of something else in their lives. Added to this is the fact that some accident-prone persons have an unconscious desire to be punished or suffer because of guilt.

God's answer to our guilt is not denying its reality or calling for self-punishment, but forgiveness. The Lord offers this forgiveness and in his forgiveness it becomes possible for us to forgive ourselves. Guilt is never really removed until it is forgiven. Harry Emerson Fosdick wrote: "No man's sin is ever done with until it comes through this process of forgiveness. Either your sin has been forgiven or else it is yet in you as sin."[13]

Shakespeare captured the inner hell and torment of unresolved guilt in his portrayal of Lady Macbeth who conspired in the murder of King Duncan. In the grip of guilt she symbolically washed her hands over and over. "It is an accustomed action with her, to seem thus washing her hands: I have known her to continue in this a quarter of an hour."[14] But that compulsive washing failed to cleanse her of guilt. Lady Macbeth wails: "Here's the smell of blood still: all the perfumes of Arabia will not sweeten this little hand. Oh, oh, oh!"[15]

What we cannot do for ourselves in removing the burden of guilt, the Lord does for us in the grace of his forgiveness. Two observations are in order about this forgiveness.

First, forgiveness doesn't cancel the consequences of the failure. Even though the deed is forgiven, it continues to pay dividends. As George Eliot's *Adam Bede* said it, "It's like a bit o' bad workmanship—you never see th' end o' th' mischief it'll do." Sin leaves its scars, and these remain after the healing of forgiveness.

Second, God's forgiveness is available to you. The message of the Bible is that "If we confess our sins, he [God] is faithful and just to forgive us our sins, and to cleanse us from all unrighteousness" (1 John 1:9). There is no sin, failure, or mistake the Lord will not forgive if you sincerely come to him, seeking his forgiveness.

When God forgives us, we can do the same for ourselves. After all, who am I to continue to indict myself if the Lord has forgiven me? If he, whose standards are so much higher than mine, forgives me, who am I to refuse to do the same? In this complete forgiveness we are then free to face the challenges of today unencumbered by the dead weight of guilt because of yesterday's failures.

Conclusions

We don't live perfect lives because none of us are perfect people. The imperfections of our being often make expression in our behavior. We make mistakes. We fall short of goals. We commit sins. Sometimes we even transform our lives into one awful mess.

Regrettably, these blunders and failures are sometimes concretized—they are forever set with no possibility of a second chance. However, when life doesn't give us a second chance it doesn't mean that it's all over for us. We can conquer regret and remorse and shake our spirits free of that awesome frustration these produce.

Notes

1. George Bernard Shaw, *St. Joan* (Scene VI), *Seven Plays* (New York: Dodd, Mead & Company, 1966), p. 893.

2. Roger H. Crook, *How to be Nervous and Enjoy It* (Nashville: Broadman Press, 1975), p. 103.

3. John R. Claypool, *Problems, Compassion, and Hope* (printed sermon, Northminster Baptist Church, Jackson, Mississippi, September 26, 1980).

4. Omar Khyyam, *The Rubaiyat of Omar Khyyam,* Stanza LI.

5. Merrill T. Eaton, Jr., and Margaret H. Peterson, *Psychiatry* (New York: Medical Examination Publishing Co., 1969); Philip Solomon and Vernon D. Patch, *Handbook of Psychiatry,* Third Edition (Lange Medical Publications, 1974), p. 333.

6. Gary R. Collins, *Overcoming Anxiety* (Santa Anna: Vision House Publishers, 1973).

7. Minirth and Meier, *Happiness Is a Choice,* p. 33.

8. Ibid., p. 33.

9. James C. Coleman, *Abnormal Psychology and Modern Life* (Glenview, IL: Scott, Foresman & Co., 1976), p. 744.

10. Walker, *Power to Manage Yourself,* p. 26.

11. Cecil Osborne, *The Art of Understanding Yourself* (Grand Rapids: Zondervan Publishing House, 1967), p. 99.

12. Ibid., p. 100.

13. Harry Emerson Fosdick, *The Secret of Victorious Living* (New York: Harper Chapel Books, Harper & Row, Publishers, 1966), p. 92.

14. William Shakespeare, *Macbeth,* Act V, Scene 1.

15. Ibid.

8

The Rat Race Revitalized

A well-to-do man in Paris, France, grew increasingly bored with the petty routine of everyday living. He finally reached the point of despair where he took his own life. Before he rushed out into eternity, he penned these words which now appear on his tombstone: "Tired of This Eternal Buttoning and Unbuttoning."

Life is often described as a rat race. It can easily become a monotonous routine of buttoning and unbuttoning; of getting up to go to work; of coming home; only to repeat the process the next day. For some, the routine of life is expressed in the lines:

> I work, work, work without end,
> Why and for whom I know not,
> I care not, I ask not.
> I am a machine.[1]

So many people feel that their life is just like that—the same thing over and over again. There is the former beauty queen who now stands on varicose-veined legs. She cleans the same house, tends to the same children, and faces the same frustrations, day in and day out. Her husband, with a gray-flannel complexion and the evidence that he's losing the battle of the bulge, is but a small cog in the corporation machinery. His dream of making it to the top has faded, along with his youth and vigor. Now he simply fights a daily battle to hold on and make do.

There is the blue-collar worker who does his nine-to-five shift at the same machine in the same factory every day. He pulls the same lever and pushes the same button, producing the same small brace in the same product he rarely sees in completed form and could never afford. He goes home to a houseful of kids and a nagging wife who, because of her frustrations, has every reason to gripe.

These are not pretty pictures of Mr. and Mrs. America. They are certainly not the scenes we see in advertisements or the portrayals on the soap operas. But they are true pictures of life as it is for millions of people in this land of vast opportunities. What has become of the American dream for them? The answer is both simple and sad. Life has become a rat race which they feel they are doomed to run, but can never win. So these millions live in a state of almost perpetual frustration. People are frustrated at work, frustrated at home, frustrated over the economy and inflation, frustrated by failures, frustrated by the constant demand to change and adapt to new ways, and just plain frustrated at being frustrated. The result for the frustrated people is that their lives lack luster, they plod with no purpose, and their death means defeat.

Let's face it—so many of these things that frustrate us aren't going to change. I recommended earlier that when life seems hopeless we must resolve to do something. Part of that resolve is an attempt to change things for the better. Without desiring to sound pessimistic, we frankly recognize that there is little we can do to change some situations. In spite of our strongest desires and best efforts, what is, often will continue to be.

Therefore, instead of changing the factors which produce our frustrations, we must do something about our attitude toward them. Life is often a rat race, and in some ways it will be that to the end. In fact, it has always been that to some degree. Genesis 5 declares the life story of generations with the monotonous repetition, "Born, begat, and died." Our hope and challenge then is not to find an exit ramp from the rat race thoroughfare, but instead to discover ways to revitalize the rat race.

It is possible to revitalize your own rat race if you will change your attitudes and correct your actions.

Change Attitudes

Frustration is a state of mind and attitudes are simply mental postures, or the way we think about something. In a real sense, the battle with frustration is fought in the mind. That which makes the difference is the attitude a person has.

Walking through the lobby of a hotel where I was staying, I saw a sign which announced an "Attitude Adjustment Period." The sign was at the door of the hotel lounge, and it announced the "happy hour." Attitude adjustment is needed, though not in the manner suggested by the sign.

When it comes down to the bottom line, we must accept the fact that there is no way out of the rat race. Life is daily and the dailiness of it involves routine. All of us must do the same things over and over again. Our need then is not to escape the rat race, but to change our attitude toward it. After all, that daily routine is productive and has positive results. Howard Upton wrote: "It is one

thing for a man to recognize the annoyances and inade-
quacies of his mode of existence, but it is something else
for him to assume that these defects render the whole
fabric of his life worthless."[2]

Because of the nature of my work, I frequently come
into contact with people who are out of the rat race, so to
speak. Each Sunday morning I preach to a congregation
of senior citizens. They are residents in an extended-care
facility in our city. They know nothing about the daily
nine-to-five grind with its wear and tear on the nerves.
They have no dishes to wash, beds to make, or children to
watch. Traffic jams at the rush hour, long lines at the
checkout counter, poor work by an employee, or meeting
deadlines aren't a part of their world. After seeing someone sitting alone in a wheelchair, not really sure which day
of the week it is, I discover that my rat race isn't that bad
after all.

Our work, whether at home or on the job, is the rat race
that frustrates many of us. That work is essential—where
would you be without your job? So, we need a change of
attitude about work.

First, recognize that work is a part of God's plan for
life. When the Lord God created man and put him in the
Garden of Eden, He gave man a work to do. "And the
Lord God took the man, and put him into the garden of
Eden to dress it and to keep it" (Gen. 2:15).

The Ten Commandments have become the basis and
foundation for the laws governing life in our Judeo-Chris-
tian society. The Fourth Commandment focuses on worship and rest. It also contains a direct command to work.
"Six days shalt thou labour, and do all thy work" (Ex.
20:9).

The apostle Paul admonished Gentile Christians in Asia, "Let him that stole steal no more: but rather let him labour, working with his hands the thing which is good" (Eph. 4:28). He also reprimanded those in Thessalonica who refused to work. "For even when we were with you, this we commanded you, that if any would not work, neither should he eat. For we hear that there are some which walk among you disorderly, working not at all, but are busybodies. Now them that are such we commend and exhort by our Lord Jesus Christ, that with quietness they work, and eat their own bread" (2 Thess. 3:10-12).

The Bible contains a strong work ethic. Man needs a work to do, and the Lord not only gives man time in which to work; he commands him to do it. Obviously work is essential from an economic standpoint. It is also essential for it is a part of God's plan for man. Even though our work can become monotonous and routine, it is to be viewed as God's will for life.

Second, we can change our attitude by seeing the higher service in our work. Since work is a phase of life God planned for us, our work then becomes something we do for God. I have heard that Ruth Graham, the wife of the famous evangelist, has a plaque over her kitchen sink which reads, "Divine services performed here three times daily." That plaque captures the meaning of Paul's words in Colossians 3:23: "And whatsoever ye do, do it heartily, as to the Lord, and not unto men."

A man was walking by a construction site where a new church building was to be erected. He saw three workmen digging for the foundation. "What are you men doing?" he asked. One man answered, "I'm digging a hole." The second responded, "I'm earning a living." The third proudly said, "I'm helping to build a cathedral." Each of the three was doing the same task, but obviously for different reasons. Which of the three was probably enjoying his work most and doing it best?

Dr. Paul Tournier wrote about a German-Swiss domestic servant who testified to him, "Since I have been sweeping my floor with Jesus, I never forget to sweep under the mat."[3]

The job you have may be mundane and unglamorous. If so, you have plenty of company. In a complex society like ours, there must be a host of people who make doorknobs, repair appliances, work at sewing machines, mop floors, and perform countless other tasks that are taken for granted. Because of the routineness of what you do, you may well feel that you are caught in a rat race designed to wear you down. But suppose you start looking at your job, routine as it is, as a service rendered for God—a divine service, if you please. I believe that such a change in attitude will go a long way toward revitalizing your rat race.

Correct Actions

The second big step to take in revitalizing the rat race of your life concerns conduct. Not only must the attitude about work be changed; some actions need to be corrected. Life must include work, but it's not to be all work. Dr. Gary Collins recommends, "Make life as balanced and meaningful as you can. Your work is only a part of your life. It shouldn't be allowed to control everything you do, nor should it be permitted to drag you down into perpetual misery."[4] In order to make life balanced and meaningful, a person must make some corrections. I recommend five corrections which will help us revitalize our own rat race.

First, reorder your priorities. What is the most important aspect in life? Many people would answer that question, "To get ahead in the world." Others would simply answer, "Success." Both of these are the outgrowth of a work ethic which places a premium on achievement. Our quest for success has made work all-important. It is the great American god. Tournier writes, "Bourgeois society has made an idol of work."[5] In fact, we even tend to measure our worth as a person in terms of our work and how well we do it. "To justify our existence and prove to ourselves that we are valuable people, we assume that we must succeed on the job. If we don't succeed at work, so the myth goes, then maybe we aren't worth much as persons."[6]

There is a certain thrill in success. There is immense satisfaction in doing a job well. In fact, Emerson remarked that the greatest satisfaction in a job well done is having done it. The excitement of accomplishment makes it all worthwhile. However, there are more important considerations. There is the joy of family, the love of a mate, the excitement of children at play, the beauty of a sunset, and time alone with God.

Second, make a change. There will be some things about a person's work which are disagreeable to him. The job hasn't been invented yet which is all peaches and cream. Sometimes we are guilty of allowing those few negative factors in our work to overshadow all the good things. Yet, some people discover that there are more things about their work which they don't like than things they enjoy.

In an English factory, all the men pushed their wheelbarrows except one slow worker who pulled his. A visitor asked the foreman why. "Oh, him," the foreman shrugged, "he hates the sight·of the blooming thing."

Some surveys reveal that more than half the people interviewed don't like their jobs. The reasons for this dislike vary, but they extend beyond inadequate pay, poor working conditions, and the lack of opportunity to advance.[7] If the dislikes outweigh the likes, a person should make a change.

Changing professions or jobs has become a rather common occurrence in America. Edgar H. Schien pointed out that roughly one half of all employees hired out of college quit their jobs and move elsewhere within five years.[8] Added to these are business executives and professional people with years of seniority and experience who resign to begin new lives and careers. I heard of one college president who, during the campus unrest in the sixties, left his post and became a taxicab driver.

Life in this world is too short and a person's worth is too important to invest year after year in a job or profession one doesn't like or enjoy. Work occupies too much of our time and energy to be hated or disliked. Even though such a major decision as changing careers at mid-life is not to be made precipitously, making a change is a viable means of revitalizing life.

Third, take a break. The problem with many people caught in the rat race is that they don't stop to rest. The Lord Jesus once told his disciples, "Come with me by yourselves to a quiet place and get some rest" (Mark 6:31, NIV). Even though the Lord's admonition in that setting didn't relate to the rat race of life, it is nonetheless excellent advice fcr every busy person.

We were made to work—but not all the time—and not without taking time out to rest. One purpose in the sabbath was to furnish a time for both man and beast to rest from labor (Ex. 20:10). The person who works seven days a week and goes way beyond acceptable limits each day is not only injuring his health and neglecting his family, he is also diminishing his efficiency as a worker.

A recognized authority on stress, Dr. Hans Selye, wrote that, "No one part of the body must be disproportionately over-worked for a long time."[9] Even the Lord God rested on the seventh day after creation.

My own work involves demanding schedules, and often I have to meet inflexible deadlines. These require that some weeks I have to spend more time working than I would like. I have discovered, though, that a brief break has great benefits. Not only does this provide moments away from the demands of work, but when I get back to it, I am able to do a better job.

Dr. Barr Taylor, assistant professor of psychiatry at Stanford University and associate director of Stanford's Laboratory for the Study of Behavioral Medicine, recommends the following: (1) Take coffee breaks—and use them to relax and clear your mind; (2) take five-minutes relaxation breaks each morning and afternoon. Use them to think of peaceful things such as a favorite vacation spot; (3) allow yourself distractions. Hang a picture of a peaceful setting on your office wall and indulge in daydreaming about it for a few minutes; (4) take time off regularly.[10]

Alan Lakein told about a woman whose time was consumed by a four-year-old daughter. No sooner did the woman sit down to read than the child appeared with some request for the mother's time and energy. The woman decided to set aside thirty minutes each day for herself. She put a lock on her bedroom door, set the kitchen timer, and sent the child to her own room to play with the promise that the mother would be available in thirty minutes. The woman then went to her room, locked the door, and sat down to read. It took the child a few days to adjust to the mother's quiet time, but the break paid off for the woman.[11]

Fourth, learn to play. The old adage goes, "All work and no play makes Jack a dull boy." The reason so many people feel worn down to the nub by the daily grind of life is that they don't take time to play.

Leisure has become a major concern in America. Some television commercials describe the weekend as the playtime. There is increasing talk about the four-day work week which will add to the leisure time available. However, some people don't play in the time they now have. Instead, they use large segments of it to sit in front of a television set. This is certainly not playing.

Everyone should have some sort of activity which provides both exercise and enjoyment. This is beneficial for good health and adds spice to living—especially when the activity involves family and friends. Whatever you choose to do for play must be something that involves your mind and not merely your body. I like to walk and run. I have found it to be good exercise as well as being enjoyable. But I have one problem: keeping my mind away from my work. It is necessary for me to keep telling myself to look and think about sights and sounds around me instead of something relating to work.

Fifth, engage in praise. Behavioral scientists recognize that actions affect attitudes. Of course, the opposite can be true as well. When we feel blue, we usually don't feel like doing anything. But we can change the attitude by acting like we want to feel. The person who makes it a point to act positively will soon feel the same way.

Beyond doubt, one reason life is such a rat race for some is that they have lost sight of priorities. This is illustrated by studies revealing how we spend our time. One study states that the average American who lives seventy years will spend these years as follows: eleven years working; eight years playing; six years eating; five and one-half years grooming; three years being educated; three years reading; three years talking; and one-half year worshiping.[12] With so little of life given to praise, it is little wonder that for some life seems to be a rat race.

No one had more cause to be discouraged than Paul the apostle. In writing to the Philippians, he didn't exhibit that disposition, though. He said, "For I have learned, in whatsoever state I am, therewith to be content" (4:11). The reason behind such a spirit was his own conduct. Paul rejoiced in all situations (1:18), and he told the Philippians, "Rejoice in the Lord alway: and again I say, Rejoice" (4:4).

The ancient psalmist wrote, "This is the day which the Lord hath made; we will rejoice and be glad in it" (118:24). Such an attitude about life transforms any day from gloom to gladness.

The minister of a quarter-time church arrived after dark at the home where he was to spend the night. The next morning he awoke to find printing on the window in the room where he had slept. He read these word, "This is the day." At breakfast, he asked his widowed hostess the meaning of the words.

She answered, "I went through a difficult and trying

time in my life. I experienced a tremendous loss and life became meaningless. When I woke up in the morning, I thought I couldn't get through the day, and when I went to bed at night I prayed that I wouldn't wake up the next morning." She told the minister that one day she came across Psalm 118:24. This brought about a complete change in her life. The woman then realized that God didn't want her to endure each day, but really to live it. She printed the words on that windowpane on the east side of her house so each morning she could watch the sun rise and be reminded that "This is the day."

Praise is one of the most vital acts for revitalizing your rat race. The benefit of faith and religion is recognized by psychiatrists and psychologists. The person who takes time for God, worship and Bible study at church, and for praise during each day of the week will find welcome release from the strains and stresses of daily living and work.

Conclusion

Life has its monotonous routines. Life can often seem like a rat race. Yet, that rat race can be revitalized. If we will change attitudes and correct actions, we will discover that the old rat race isn't so bad after all.

The French painter, Pierre Auguste Renoir, suffered from arthritis in later life. A friend once watched Renoir at work, seeing how he held the brush with his fingertips. He saw that each movement of the artist's hands caused him pain. The friend asked why he kept painting when the pain was so great. Renoir answered, "The pain passes, but the beauty remains."

Multitudes of people experience the pain of frustration

in their daily work and responsibilities. However, there is also the possibility of beauty in these. The rat race is not all bad. So, by seeing the good in it, as well as doing what we can to make it more enjoyable, the daily routine of life can become a beautiful experience with lasting values.

Notes

1. Quoted from *American Chronicle* by Ray Stannard Baker (New York: Charles Scribner's Sons, 1945), p. 181.

2. Howard Upton, "In Defense of the Old Rat Race," *The Art of Living* (New York: Berkley Books, 1980), p. 214.

3. Paul Tournier, *The Adventure of Living* (New York: Harper & Row, 1965), p. 225.

4. Collins, *You Can Profit from Stress,* p. 126.

5. Tournier, *The Adventure of Living,* p. 60.

6. Collins, *You Can Profit from Stress,* p. 118.

7. Ibid., p. 116.

8. Edgar H. Schien, "The First Job Dilemma," *Psychology Today* (March, 1968), pp. 26-37.

9. Hans Selye, *The Stress of Life* (New York: McGraw-Hill, 1956), p. 266.

10. Chuck Michelini, "Top Experts' No. 1 Plan to Beat Stress," *National Inquirer* (May 20, 1980), p. 37.

11. Alan Lakein, *How to Get Control of Your Time and Your Life* (New York: A Signet Book, 1973), pp. 91-92.

12. *Tarbell's Teacher's Guide,* 1980-81, edited by Frank S. Mead (Old Tappan, NJ: Fleming H. Revell Co., 1980), p. 46.

9

How to Get On Top of Life

An attorney friend of mine lives in our town. He isn't a member of my congregation, but I meet him frequently at club meetings, civic and social events, as well as at a favorite coffee place. When I see him, I usually ask, "How are you doing today, Counselor?" The answer he gives without fail is, "Fairly well, under the circumstances."

A senior minister met a new, young minister. The older minister asked, "How are you doing?"

The young man responded, "Very well, thank you, under the circumstances."

"Under the circumstances!" thundered the senior minister. "What are you doing under the circumstances? Man, get on top of the circumstances!"

How frequently we feel "under the circumstances." This is certainly true when we are frustrated. To say the least, when we experience the mental state of frustration we surely don't feel on top of the world. Just the opposite!

I believe we can get on top of life regardless of what our circumstances may be. In fact, I believe we're not supposed to be the victims of the circumstances of life—we're to be victors over those circumstances. I'm not indicating that we can keep the undesirable events from the door of our lives. Such is impossible. Things happen every day over which we have no control. We can't keep them from happening, but we don't have to be victims of these circumstances, pressed down and crushed by them. It's possible for us to be victors over them. In other words, regardless of what our situation may be, we can get on top of life.

The chapters of this book have addressed various facets of frustration. These chapters have been written from the perspective of stating a frustration problem and attempting to offer some solutions. This chapter is different. I want us to look at the life of a man who definitely was down and out but who was helped to get on top of life. In seeing how he managed it, we, too, can discover ways to become victors in life.

The man's story is told in the New Testament. Listen to it:

> Now there is at Jerusalem by the sheep market a pool, which is called in the Hebrew tongue Bethesda, having five porches. In these lay a great multitude of impotent folk, of blind, halt, withered, waiting for the moving of the water. For an angel went down at a certain season into the pool, and troubled the water: whosoever then first after the troubling of the water stepped in was made whole of whatsoever disease he had. And a certain man was there, which had an infirmity thirty and eight years. When Jesus saw him lie, and knew that he had been now a long time in that case, he saith unto him, Wilt thou be made whole? The impotent man answered him, Sir, I have no man, when the water is troubled, to put me into the pool: but when I am coming, another steppeth down before me. Jesus saith unto him, Rise, take up thy bed, and walk. And immediately the man was made whole, and took up his bed, and walked (John 5:2-9).

Here was a man who was "under the circumstances," but who got on top of life. Notice that he was chained to the past, challenged by a possibility, and called to a performance. These three facts about him speak to our needs, for in dealing with people about life I often meet people who need to break the chains to the past, be challenged by possibilities within their reach, and respond to a call to perform.

Chained to the Past

Two statements in the story about the man underscore the fact that he was chained to the past. First, he had suffered his infirmity for thirty-eight years. We have no idea how old the man was at the time he met Jesus, but even by today's average life span, thirty-eight years is more than half a lifetime. For thirty-eight years this man had suffered from his affliction.

Second, when the Lord saw the infirm man, Jesus recognized that he had been there for a long time. The man's presence in that place had become permanent. He had become a fixture—a part of the scenery. The fact that he had been ill for thirty-eight years and in that place for a long time both emphasize that he was a man chained to his past. All of his todays were but monotonous repetitions of his yesterdays.

There are many people today who are also chained to the past. For them, today is just a carbon copy of yesterday. One New Year's Eve I preached a sermon on the theme, "Will It Be a New Year?" On that Sunday evening people were wishing each other a happy new year. But would it really be a new year for many of them? I did not mean a new year in *time,* for obviously the old year would pass into history, to be replaced by a new one. But would it be a new year in *kind?* Would it be a different kind of year; a year of moving forward in the journey of life rather than remaining rooted in the same spot?

Eugene O'Neill's *Moon for the Misbegotten* depicts James Tyrone, a failed actor and owner of a small farm rented by the Hogans. Tyrone, trying to forget his guilt and failure through alcoholism, cries one night to Josie Hogan, "No present, no future. Only the past happening over and over again now."

I read about a man who graduated from college at the top of his class. He was quickly enlisted for a teaching position in a school system and taught there for ten years. Then the position of principal became vacant. The man applied for the job, but another person with fewer years in service was chosen for the job. The man was outraged and went to the superintendent of schools. The teacher asked, "Why wasn't I chosen for the job of principal? I've got ten years of experience teaching in this school, yet you chose someone with less experience than I!" The superintendent responded, "You're my friend, and I don't want to hurt your feelings, but I must correct you. You don't have ten years experience here. You've got one year's experience repeated nine times."

If we are to get on top of life, we first must break the chains with the past. We must close the book on yesterday, leaving behind both the good and the bad to move on to the prospects for today.

A pastor went to the office of one of the members of his congregation. They had a supper engagement and had agreed to meet at the man's office. As the pastor waited for the man to finish his last item of business, he glanced around the office and saw a wastepaper basket by the door. He commented to the man, "That's a peculiar place to have a wastepaper basket."

The man responded, "That's the most important thing in my office," and continued working with no further explanation. When the man was finished with his work and ready to leave, he walked over to the basket by the door. Above it on the wall was a calendar with a page for each day in the year. The man tore off the page representing that day and stood looking at it in silence. Then he bowed his head and closed his eyes. After a few moments he opened his eyes, crumpled the page from the calendar into a wad, and threw it into the wastepaper basket.

As they left the office, the preacher asked the man to explain what he had just done. The man responded, "Preacher, that's my ritual at the end of each day. I tear the page off the calendar representing the day and look at it, thinking of all that day has been for me—the successes, the mistakes. Then I ask God to forgive me for when I was wrong and thank him for helping me do some things right. When I'm through, I wad up that page and throw it away, symbolizing for me that the day is done and I'm finished with it. Now I'm ready to face tomorrow without the dead weight of today."

If we're to get on top of life, we must break the chains with the past. As long as we're moored to the yesterdays of our lives, we'll never be equal to today.

Challenged By a Possibility

When Jesus spoke to the man by the pool, he asked him a very strange question. The Master asked, "Wilt thou be made whole?" or "Do you want to be healed?" (RSV).

That seems a strange question to ask a man who has been sick for thirty-eight long, weary years. But the Lord asked the question for a very good reason. He did so to revive the man's hope.

Those thirty-eight years must have been long and disappointing. Doubtless in the early days of his infirmity the man had high hopes for a cure. As he saw other people healed, he thought, *Soon it will be my time—one day I, too, will be healed.* But day followed day in the seemingly endless march of time, until thirty-eight years had passed and he was still crippled. The man had doubtless given up all hope of being anything other than what he was—a man under the circumstances of life rather than on top of them. There was even a note of resignation in his voice when he answered Jesus. "Sir, I have no man, . . . to put me in the pool."

The question, "Do you want to be healed?" was designed to challenge him with a possibility. Jesus was saying, "You are the way you are, but you don't have to stay that way if you don't want to. You can be different than you are."

The fact that life can be changed for the better is the essence of the gospel. We talk about the gospel being good news. One facet of that good news is that life can become better than it is. Paul emphasized this fact when he wrote: "When anyone is joined to Christ, he is a new being; the old is gone, the new has come" (2 Cor. 5:17, TEV). Jesus called fisherman brothers, "Come ye after me, and I will make you to become fishers of men" (Mark 1:17). The word *become* says that life becomes better when one begins to follow Christ.

We're so quick to say that something is impossible.

Some believe that they are doomed to remain what they are—victims of circumstances rather than becoming victors over circumstances. Dr. James Mallory observed:

> Actually, many people have a *negative* faith. They *believe* all right, but they believe the wrong things. They believe that they are the way they are because they were "just born that way." They believe that they will be as they are now until the day they die. Far from lacking faith, they have strong faith. And their faith is producing the very negative and destructive things that make them and their loved ones unhappy.[1]

We need to be challenged by the possibilities of life. Admiral Hyman Rickover, the father of the nuclear submarine, is a visionary scientist. However, he's had to contend with negative-minded men and nay-sayers. One day Admiral Rickover had the words, "It can't be done," printed on a card in gray ink. The card was circulated among his staff. They read the words, "It can't be done," and then found on the other side in bold black ink these words, "But here it is!" How many times have people said, "It can't be done," and then someone did it?

Ralph W. Sockman in *The Highway of God* tells about Arthur Rubinstein visiting in New York City. He was invited to church by a friend. The famous concert pianist responded, "Yes, I will go if you take me to hear a preacher who will tempt me to do the impossible." Ralph Waldo Emerson said, "Neither you nor the world knows what you can do until you have tried."

A quadruple amputee was carried into a veterans' hospital. Even the case-hardened staff was shaken at the sight of the young Vietnam veteran. He appeared to be a broken, useless relic with four grotesque stumps instead of two arms and two legs. He was only twenty-two, but the doctors were sure he would spend the rest of his life in institutions, labeled a "basket case." Psychiatrists and case workers worried about him because they knew men in his condition frequently lose the will to live. Furthermore, when a man feels like a burden and a problem, his life expectancy drops.

This amputee, however, surprised everyone. He asked his hospital roommate to look in his locker and get his New Testament. "Now," instructed the young amputee, "open it to John 3:16, and read it to me." When the friend did, the young veteran said, "I am *whosoever*."

He didn't slip into depression and die a slow death. Instead, he became a source of inspiration to all who entered his room. Eventually he was fitted with artificial limbs and discharged from the hospital. A year later the young amputee, who everyone thought would be institutionalized until he died, married one of his nurses! Everyone had been ready to sign his death certificate, but he had caught sight of what was possible for him.

Did you ever hear the fable about the frog? He was hopping along a dirt road when he landed in the middle of a deep rut. He hopped to get out of the rut, but he couldn't make it. His frog friends came and shouted down encouragements to him from the top of the rut. But the little frog said, "I just can't do it. The rut is too deep and my hop is too short." So his frog friends left him and went on their way. But the next day one of the frogs came along and found the little frog hopping happily along the road. "I thought you were in a rut and couldn't get out," said his friend. "I was," replied the little frog, "but then a big truck came along and I had to get out.''

We can do more than we give ourselves credit for. If we are ever to get out from under the circumstances and on top of life, we need to be challenged by the possibility of what can be. Jesus asked the man, "Do you want to be healed?" He challenged him to the possibility of healing.

Called to a Performance

Finally the Lord Jesus told the man, "Rise, take up thy bed, and walk." He called the man to do something for himself. Those thirty-eight years he had been lying there had been spent waiting for someone to come and help him. When Jesus asked him if he wanted to be healed, he responded, "Sir, I have no man." He was saying, "I can't be healed because no one will come and help me." In effect, the Master told him, "You get up. Do something for yourself!"

This brings us to the heart of the matter about getting on top of life. How many people, who are pressed down by life's circumstances, are waiting for someone to come along and lift them up? They don't want to be on the bottom—they want to be on the top of life. But instead of doing anything about it themselves, they are like the man by the pool, waiting for someone else to come along and do it for them. But we must do something for ourselves if the possibilities are to become realities.

What are we to do for ourselves in order to get on top of life? Look at what Jesus told that man, for in his commands to him we discover some pertinent performances required of us if we are to get on top of life.

First, Jesus called the man to "Rise." The man was flat on his back, and he was wallowing in self-pity. I imagine his response to Jesus' question about his desire to be healed, "I have no man," was almost a whine in which he conveyed the feeling, "poor little me."

All of us have experienced self-pity; some of us more than others. When life goes contrary to our wishes and desires, it is so easy for us to feel we're the only person who has it rough. But one of the sad facts about self-pity is that while we're rolling in it, we're not doing anything to get out of it. George Weinberg wrote that self-pity "invites you to stand still and ask, 'Why me?' instead of figuring out the best place to go from here."[2] He added, "You can help yourself. But only if you stop feeling sorry for yourself."[3]

Therefore, the first positive move we must make in order to get on top of life is to rise from the slough of self-pity. Quit fishing for sympathy and start doing something about your circumstances.

Second, Jesus called the man to "Take up thy bed." In essence the Lord was saying, "Do what God gives you the power to do." The man could and did take up his pallet because Jesus healed him. The power of God experienced in the healing made it possible for him to get up.

We must recognize that we are not all-powerful. I'm impressed by the self-help books which tell me that I can do anything. I like the P.M.A. philosophy—the positive mental attitude approach to life. We often sell ourselves short and don't realize we can do more than we do. But there's a limit to what I can do. I can't do everything I might want to do. My ability is not adequate for all the challenges and demands of life.

A father was trying to impress his son with the fact that he could do more than he was doing. He stressed the fact that the boy could do anything he set his mind to do. Then the father asked, "Son, can you think of one thing you can't do if you really tried?" The boy responded, "Yeah. Have you ever tried to put the toothpaste back in the tube?"

What we must realize is that we can do whatever must be done by us if we avail ourselves of the strength God offers. One of my favorite verses is Paul's personal testimony to the Philippians: "I can do all things through Christ which strengtheneth me" (4:13). I've been impressed by the fact that the verse begins and ends with first person singular pronouns—"I" and "me." This emphasizes the fact that I'm not to sit back and wait for someone else to do for me what I'm to do for myself. However, the secret to doing "all things" is not the first person singular pronouns with which the verse begins and ends, but the Christ in the center of the verse. The Lord is the one who gives me the strength to do what I must do. A beautiful scroll hanging in my office reminds me: "Lord, help me to remember that nothing is going to happen today that you and I together cannot handle."

In counseling with people who feel they can't go on because of some trauma or crisis in life, I have prescribed Philippians 4:13 as a spiritual vitamin to be taken in massive doses each day. Keep saying over and over, "I can do all things in him who strengthens me" (RSV).

Third, Jesus called the man to "walk." It wasn't enough for him to get up and take up his pallet. He was to begin going places and doing things. For thirty-eight years the cripple had lain by the pool—going nowhere, doing nothing. Now he was to get on with the business of living.

If we are to get on top of life, we must not only rise from the bed of self-pity and do what God gives us the power to do; we must move toward goals. One of the greatest handicaps many people have in life is that they have no goals. Albert Camus, the French Nobel Prize winner, said that life is absurd. He saw no reason behind or beyond it. Even though I disagree with him, I must admit that many people live absurd lives. They live a merry-go-round existence of rushing around and around, but never really going anywhere.

Life often becomes an endurance contest of just getting through day after day because there are no goals in living. Someone said, "Everyone needs long-range goals if for no other reason than to keep from being frustrated by short-range failures."[4]

Conclusion

Perhaps you are in the same fix as my attorney friend. You are doing fairly well, under the circumstances. Maybe you are one of the millions who live life daily under the circumstances, instead of on top of them. You look at the frustrations, disappointments, and troubles in life from the bottom side, for you are always under them.

I believe that it's possible for us to be on top of life. This doesn't mean that we won't experience frustrations, disappointments, and troubles. None of us is so fleet of foot that we can successfully outrun these facts of life. However, we don't have to be victims of life's circumstances. We can be victors over circumstances! This is what the Lord Jesus made possible for a man in the long ago. He can do the same thing for us in the here and now.

Notes

1. Mallory, *The Kink and I,* p. 214.
2. George Weinberg, *Self Creation* (New York: St. Martins Press, 1978), p. 188.
3. Ibid.
4. *Bits and Pieces,* Marvin G. Gregory, Ed. (Fairfield, NJ: Economics Press, Vol. 13, No. 7, July, 1980), p. 5.

10

God's Peace: The Ultimate Answer

A man arrived at the doctor's office for his 3:00 appointment at exactly 3:00. Because the doctor was still involved with an earlier appointment, the man had to wait. In fact, he had to wait all of five minutes. He spent the time pacing the reception area like a caged animal, looking at his watch every thirty seconds.

When he was finally summoned to the examining room, the doctor said, "Sit down, please." The man sharply responded, "I don't have time to sit down! I'm too busy!"

"If you want me to examine you, sit down!" replied the doctor.

When the man sat down the physician asked, "Now, what seems to be the trouble?"

The patient answered, "Doc, I've got troubles everywhere I look. I've got troubles in my business; troubles at home; troubles, everywhere—and I'm just plain run-down!"

The physician proceeded with the examination, listening to the man's pulse beat, taking his blood pressure—doing the usual poking, probing, and puncturing. When he had finished, the physician said to the patient, "You're not run-down. Just the opposite—you're wound up!"

The man responded, "Well, Doc, give me something to slow me down then."

"What do you want?" asked the doctor.

"Give me a tranquilizer, or something."

"Very well," responded the doctor as he sat down and began writing a prescription.

The man took the prescription and stuck it in his pocket without looking at it. He rushed off to the neighborhood drugstore to get the prescription filled.

The pharmacist looked at the prescription and said to the man, "I'm sorry, but I can't fill this prescription."

"What do you mean, you can't fill that prescription!" retorted the man. "This is a drugstore, isn't it? You are a pharmacist, aren't you? That's a doctor's prescription, so why can't you fill it?"

The pharmacist answered, "I'm sorry, sir, but we don't stock this in our store. If you want this prescription filled, go home and get your Bible."

The man looked at the prescription for the first time and read: "Take three doses of Colossians 3:15 every day." He went home and looked up the verse in his Bible. It reads: "And let the peace of God rule in your hearts."

Immediately, the man called the doctor and asked, "What do you mean by this prescription?"

The physician answered, "Your real trouble is spiritual, not physical. What you need is peace. I can't give it to you; the pharmacist can't give it to you; only God can give you peace."

So many of us are like that man. We need a peace that only God can give. Our lives are filled with the panic and frenzy of frustrations which push us to the limit. We often follow the advice in the lines:

> When in trouble, when in doubt;
> Run in circles, scream and shout!

The ultimate answer for this frustration is to experience the peace of God. Frustration and peace are antithetical —they are exact opposites. It is virtually impossible for a person to be flustered and frustrated and at the same time be experiencing the peace of God. No room is left for frustration when the peace of God rules in the heart. The New Testament word for peace, *eirene,* describes a wholeness and oneness which is the exact opposite of the fractured and fragmented mind of the frustrated person.

The tragedy of so many of our lives is that we know frustration, but don't experience peace. When asked by some monks where he was going and what he was seeking, Dante, the Italian poet, replied, "I am searching for that which every man seeks—peace and rest." Even though we have sought it, we don't have it.

The average American lives in the most comfortable, luxuriously appointed house to be found in the world. Yet, there has never been a time when there was as much discord, frustration, stress, and tension in that house as is true today. According to national statistics, the following is true of every twelve couples in your block:

—Four will dissolve their marriage in a divorce court.

—Six will tough it out to the end, but never experience true harmony and happiness in marriage.

—Only two will come to have a meaningful and fulfilling relationship.

What a difference the peace of God would make in our homes!

Peace is absent in the home—and everywhere else as well—because there is no peace in our lives. Some folks come to church so uptight that it's almost impossible for

---

the preacher to put them to sleep anymore—even when they're sitting on comfortable, upholstered pews.

Since God's peace is the ultimate answer for our frustrations, what is this peace, how can we experience it, and what does it do for us? I believe the answers to these questions are found in Philippians 4. Paul wrote: "And the peace of God, which passeth all understanding, shall keep your hearts and minds through Christ Jesus" (v. 7).

The Sublimity of God's Peace

The first question to be addressed about God's peace is, what is it? Paul answered, it "passeth all understanding." In effect the apostle said that God's peace is sublime; that it is beyond description.

There are two possible meanings of the statement, "passeth all understanding." First, Paul may have been saying that God's peace is of such a quality or nature that man cannot duplicate or produce it himself. We can do so many great and wonderful things for ourselves. Most people have failed to come to understand the vast power within ourselves—the power to achieve; to become. But our power is limited—we are not omnipotent. There are some things we cannot do for ourselves, and these things relate to areas of our greatest needs.

Our lack of peace proves that it is not a condition we produce but a gift we must receive. Don't think men haven't tried to create peace. Quite to the contrary! Diplomats have sat for weeks in peace conferences—and all to no avail.

The Munich Conference in September 1938, was part of the policy of appeasement which preceded World War II. Representatives of England and France met with Adolph

Hitler of Germany and Benito Mussolini of Italy in Munich, Germany. England's representative was Prime Minister Neville Chamberlain. He returned from the conference in a spirit of elation and exuberance. Coming out of his airplane, Chamberlain waved the briefcase containing the Munich Pact signed by Adolph Hitler. Jubilantly Chamberlain announced to the crowd, "This means peace in our time." But before the ink on that document was dry, Europe was embroiled in war. Such has been the futility of man's efforts to achieve and experience peace. What has been true on an international scale is equally true on the national, domestic, and personal levels of life.

The peace about which Paul wrote is not something one man can produce. We cannot work out a formula, package it with detailed instructions, and then put it on the market. God's peace passes all understanding.

The second possible meaning of Paul's statement about God's peace passing all understanding is that this peace is so tremendous that it is beyond the capacity of our minds to grasp. The peace the Lord God offers cannot be fully expressed verbally or grasped mentally. All our attempts to describe and explain it fall far short of the goal. This peace is so wonderfully sublime that it surpasses the limits of our understanding.

There are so many things in this world I cannot understand. I am persuaded that the same is also true of you. I often hear people say, "I just can't understand it." Many times I have to say the same thing. When asked questions about the profundities of life, I often have to answer, "I don't know. I can't understand it."

One Sunday my son and I were riding home from church. He was about eleven at the time, and he asked me a question suggested by his Sunday School lesson that day. It was one of those questions to which God alone has the answer. I honestly replied, "Ross, I don't know." He looked at me rather hard and said, "What do you mean, you don't know! You're a preacher, you're supposed to know everything."

I certainly don't understand everything—far from it! There are so many experiences and events which leave me bewildered and confused. Furthermore, if the walls of my office had a voice, they would verify that I'm not the only one who doesn't understand a lot of things.

So it is with this great and wonderful peace of God. No one can understand it for it passes all understanding. How is it possible for one to be at peace when everything in the world and his life seems out of order? That's something which is beyond understanding. Thankfully, however, we don't have to understand God's peace in order to experience it.

The Source of God's Peace

The peace about which Paul wrote is "the peace of God." This means that it is a peace which has its source in God. It is grounded in God's presence and power.

There are "peace of mind" cults in America today. B. W. Woods wrote: "Peace of mind is presented as obtainable by rising each day with a positive outlook, memorizing a verse of Scripture, thinking good thoughts, and refusing to be discouraged."[1]

I frequently visit bookstores and spend time looking at the types and titles of books available. I'm fascinated with the self-help section in bookstores and have been impressed by the number of books dealing with the discovery of peace. Some of these books offer a neatly packaged peace plan for your life.

The peace of God, however, is not experienced as the result of following simple instructions like putting together some do it yourself article. Instead, it can only be experienced in a person—Jesus Christ. The Lord God doesn't offer a plan for peace. He does offer a person through whom we can experience peace. The Lord Jesus said: "Come unto me, all ye that labour and are heavy laden, and I will give you rest" (Matt. 11:28).

The reason so many people today don't experience the peace of God is that they don't have peace with God through Jesus Christ. Paul wrote about the possibility of this peace to the Roman Christians: "Therefore being justified by faith, we have peace with God through our Lord Jesus Christ" (Rom. 5:1). Man's spiritual alienation and separation from God is ended in Jesus Christ. When Christ is invited into the life by faith, the barriers are broken down—people then have peace with God. When we do, it is then possible to experience the peace of God.

The apostle not only wrote that God's peace has its source in him; he stated that we come to experience that peace as we concentrate our lives on him. Philippians 4:7, in which Paul described God's peace, is not to be considered in isolation. It is, in fact, the climax of what Paul began in verse 4 of that chapter. Therefore, consider the passage in its completeness.

First, *engage in the praise of the Lord.* "Rejoice in the Lord alway: and again I say, Rejoice" (v. 4). The direction of this praise is "in the Lord," and the duration of it is "alway." The word *rejoice* involves the idea of a confidence about the Lord that enables one to be hopefully optimistic regardless of his life situation or predicament.

Second, *experience the presence of the Lord*. "Lct your moderation be known unto all men. The Lord is at hand" (v. 5). All of us live daily in the presence of God, but we are not always aware of his presence. In fact, sometimes we live as if God were nowhere about. What a difference it would make in our crisis times if we realized we aren't alone—that the Lord is near!

A woman visited her old family home place, taking her small son with her. The house had been locked and deserted for years. The shutters were closed and the drapes were drawn. Even though the sun shone brightly outside, the interior of the house was almost as dark as a tomb. The little boy wandered into the parlor and saw a ray of sunlight shining through a small hole in a window shade. The sun ray splashed in a circle of bright light on the floor. The boy stood in that pool of light and called out, "Look, Mom! I'm standing in the smile of God." Daily we live in the center of God's love, and the Lord is always near.

Third, *exercise in prayer to the Lord*. "Be careful for nothing; but in every thing by prayer and supplication with thanksgiving let your requests be made known unto God" (v. 6). The word *careful* means anxious and comes from a root which means to have a divided mind. Ray Frank Robbins wrote: "It describes the mind as looking two ways and not being able to find a place where it can settle down."[2] Anxiety is a condition of concern in which one is so weighed with worry that he can do nothing. But Paul said, in effect, "Don't worry about anything, but pray about everything."

Having done these three things, then a person can *enjoy the peace of the Lord*. Verse 7 about God's peace is the climax of what Paul said in verses 4-6. Ralph Herring advised: "In this day of tension and trouble, of frustration and failure, when pressure increases to the breaking point, we shall do well to linger with these verses long enough to learn their secret."[3] This we must do, for in these verses one discovers the secret of God's peace. It is not until the Lord is so central in your life that you rejoice in him always, remembering that he is always with you, and casting your cares upon him, that you can know his peace which passes all understanding.

The prophet Isaiah said it this way: "Thou wilt keep him in perfect peace, whose mind is stayed on thee: because he trusteth in thee" (26:3). The peace that is God's ultimate answer for our frustrations comes only from him. It is experienced by us as we focus upon him. Then that peace will become the rest for which the spirit longs.

The Strength of God's Peace

What does the peace of God do for us? Paul answered that it "shall keep your hearts and minds through Christ Jesus." The word *keep (phrorein)* is a military term. It means to stand on guard, to keep watch over.

The apostle was under arrest in Rome when he wrote these words. He was under the constant surveillance of a Roman soldier. To be sure, the purpose of that guard was not to protect the apostle from harm, but to see that he didn't escape. However, Paul knew something personally about guards. He knew that guards also have a protective purpose.

Cities in ancient times were surrounded by high walls. These walls were for the purpose of protection. Sentries were posted at points along the top of the walls. The sentry's purpose was to be a lookout, watching for an approaching enemy. The people within the city could go about the normal activities of life feeling safe and secure. They were safe within the walls and protected by the patrolling sentries. The Philippian saints understood all this for their city was a Roman colony and a military outpost. They were protected by a Roman garrison.

Understand that God's peace doesn't keep all the crises, disappointments, and frustrations of life from us. Some Christians wrongly believe that just because they belong to God and seek to live for him their lives should be trouble-free. Just the opposite is the case, however. Doing what you believe is God's will can result in experiencing troubles you wouldn't have otherwise known. The fact is that crises and troubles and the frustrations they can cause are daily occurrences in life, and there is no wall high enough or strong enough to keep them out. However, the peace of God means that we have peace in the midst of these experiences. The storms rage without with all their fury and power. But in the heart and mind—the inner sanctuary—we are at peace. The heart in Paul's use is the innermost recess of our being. It is the seat of feeling, will, and thought. The mind is the area of mental activity. Together these represent the inner person. Therefore, even though dangers lurk without, crises develop with daily regularity, and life is filled with disappointments and defeats, we can experience peace. In the sanctuary of the heart and mind there is peace in Christ, for God's peace is independent of external conditions.

An unknown poet wrote:

> I know a peace where there is no peace,
> A calm where the wild winds blow.

> A secret place where, face to face
> With the Master, I may go.

Some years ago, I had an experience in which I learned the meaning of the strength of God's peace in "a calm where the wild winds blow." I was pastor of the Baptist church in the town of Gloster in southwest Mississippi. One Sunday morning an unwelcome visitor came to our community—Hurricane Hilda. We could have no church services because of the fury of the storm, resulting in streets blocked by uprooted trees and broken power lines. During the height of the storm that Sunday morning, I felt the need to go next door to the church and see if the buildings had suffered damage. It was about the time the people would normally be in the sanctuary for worship. I sat alone in that beautiful place of worship for some minutes before returning home. Outside the storm raged in its fury, doing damage to houses and business establishments. But inside that sanctuary there was a blessed peace and calm. It was not a peace away from the storm that roared, but instead a peace and calm in the very heart of the storm.

In a similar fashion the peace of God in Christ Jesus guards the heart and mind in the midst of all the storms of life.

Conclusion

There is nothing that men want more and experience less than peace. The tired housewife whose days are filled with crying babies, noisy appliances, and intruding sales people cries, "Oh, for just a little peace and quiet." The busy business executive, running from appointment to appointment in the midst of honking traffic jams and pushing sidewalk crowds, exclaims, "Oh, for just a little peace." What they are asking for is a quiet place away from the turmoil of daily life.

What we need far more than a quiet place in the rush of life is the inner peace that only God can give. We can't find that peace in the world for the world doesn't have it to offer. But we can find it in the Lord, and he is ready to fill our lives with his peace. His peace is the ultimate answer to our frustrations. You can't be frustrated and filled with God's peace at the same time, so do for yourself now what the doctor prescribed for his wound-up patient: "Let the peace of God rule in your hearts."

Notes

1. B. W. Woods, *God's Answer to Anxiety* (Nashville: Broadman Press, 1968), p. 9.

2. Ray Frank Robbins, *Philippians: Rejoice in the Lord* (Nashville: Convention Press, 1980), pp. 127-28.

3. Ralph Herring, *To Live Is Christ* (Nashville: Broadman Press, 1953), p. 98.

11

Help Yourself to Freedom from Frustration

In the previous chapters we looked at some of the faces of frustration. In doing so we recognized that frustration is a fact of life and a reality with which we must daily and repeatedly deal. We've been reminded that frustration pops up in many different areas of life, and all of us face it again and again. Hopefully, we came to see that being frustrated isn't a hopeless condition.

In one sense, I hesitate to write these closing words on the subject. Even though something in me at times cries out for pat one-two-three answers for life and living, I am also aware that something as complex and multifaceted as frustration cannot be easily dismissed with clever cliches and simplistic solutions. Nonetheless, I feel the need to try to lift from all that has been shared in the previous chapters some essential exercises which will help us to experience freedom from frustration. I do so with the hope that we can embed these exercises in our minds and program ourselves to do them whenever we feel ourselves experiencing frustration.

Regardless of the cause or the degree of your frustration, you can help yourself to freedom from it by beginning with these three essential exercises. Notice, I said begin, for each of these three exercises will open doors to a wide range of actions and adjustments in attitudes. The three exercises are: accept responsibility for your feelings, realize that there is hope for you, and decide on a plan of action and then implement it.

Accept Responsibility

The first step in gaining freedom from frustration is to accept responsibility for your feelings. Frustration is an emotion—a feeling. It is, as we have seen, a sense of dissatisfaction because of unfulfilled needs, or because of the failure to achieve goals. However, we're the only ones who can do anything about our feelings. Even though the feeling of frustration may have been prompted by a set of circumstances beyond our control, and be experienced without our consciously willing it, only we can do something about it. You can't help becoming frustrated, but you can choose to stop feeling frustrated. This won't be done, however, until you accept responsibility for how you feel. The person who says, "I can't get over this feeling of frustration," is simply saying, "I don't choose to get over this feeling—at least, not enough to do something about it."

Remember, frustration is a reaction to some disappointment or setback. By accepting responsibility for your feelings, you determine to begin responding to the situation—not reacting to it. As you learn to control your reactions and to respond rather than react, you will begin to feel better about yourself, and you will be able to discover ways to deal constructively with the frustrating situation instead of allowing it to deal destructively with you.

Realize There Is Hope

The second essential exercise in gaining freedom from frustration is the realization that there is hope, even in the midst of your frustration. The seventeenth-century English poet, Alexander Pope, wrote: "Hope springs eternal in the human breast." In spite of the poet's words, sometimes we feel completely hopeless in the midst of our frustration.

Herbert Norman, a Canadian diplomat and one-time ambassador to Egypt, was a great scholar on Japanese culture. He committed suicide in April, 1957. A crumpled note found in his coat pocket read, "I have no option. I must kill myself because I live without hope."[1] What a waste, for a person does not have to live without hope!

In spite of the severity of the situation, there is hope. The hope may be that the situation can be reversed through continued work, or that a better day and another opportunity will come, or just that we can adapt ourselves to the situation and come to profit from the experience. Added to this is the hope that we can experience God's peace. In other words, there is hope for a change—in us or in our situation.

There's an old cliché which says, "Where there's life, there's hope." When we come to see the hope that's there, our lives will be enhanced. Then we can reverse the cliché and say with psychiatrist Karl Menninger, "Where there's hope, there's life."

Decide and Act

The third essential exercise by which we can experience freedom from frustration is to decide on a plan of action and implement it. Begin by stopping long enough to take a serious look at the possible courses of action available to you. This may be to try again, or to try something new. Or, it may mean seeking to discover how you can come to terms with whatever has prompted your frustration. What it doesn't mean is giving up and thereby allowing the frustration you feel to totally paralyze your life. You have some options! You can do something! Therefore, agree on a plan of action.

Then, having decided on the best course of action, get with it! Some of the best-laid plans of men often come to naught simply because they are not implemented. Don't be like Dorothy L. Sayers's character in *Clouds of Witness* who spent his days writing a record of the things he intended to do in life. When he died at the age of ninety-six, all that was left was a chronicle of plans he'd never implemented. Having chosen the best thing to do in the midst of your frustration or the situation causing that frustration, get up and do it!

Conclusion

Having suggested these three essential exercises, let me remind you again that this freedom to which we can help ourselves isn't permanent or complete. By this I mean that we can experience freedom from a frustrating situation today, but tomorrow will present us with a whole new set of frustrating situations, and perhaps even some of the same ones we face today. Thus these suggestions for dealing with frustration are much like the doctor's instructions on a prescription—take the doses daily and several times a day. If we are diligent in doing this, we will be able to experience *freedom from frustration*.

Note

1. Quoted in A. Dudley Dennison, *Prescription for Life* (Grand Rapids: Zondervan Publishing House, 1975), p. 141.